Moments of Prayer

DAVID SCOTT

First published in Great Britain 1997
Society for Promoting Christian Knowledge
Holy Trinity Church
Marylebone Road
London NW1 4DU

Biblical quotations are from *The Revised English Bible* © 1989
Oxford and Cambridge University Presses.

Every effort has been made to trace the copyright holders of
material quoted here. Information on any omissions should be
sent to the publishers who will make full acknowledgement
in any future editions.

British Library Cataloguing-in-Publication Data
A catalogue record of this book is available
from the British Library

ISBN 0–281–04987–4

Typeset by Pioneer Associates, Perthshire
Printed in Great Britain by
The Cromwell Press, Melksham, Wiltshire

Contents

Thou wilt say that I speak too high on this matter of prayer, which is indeed no mastery nor difficulty for me to write, but it were a great mastery for a man to practice it.

Walter Hilton, *The Ladder of Perfection* (Bk. 1, ch. 33)

When you start measuring somebody, measure him right, child, measure him right. Make sure you don taken into account what hills and valleys he come through before he got to wherever he is.

Lorraine Hansberry, *A Raisin in the Sun*

—

The happiest years of my ministry were those in which, as the vicar of a great industrial parish, I was nearest to the people. Faces look out at me from the past – toil-worn faces radiant with love and confidence. Nothing of what men foolishly call success is worth comparison with the experiences which those faces recall.

Herbert Hensley Henson, *Ad Clerum*

The beginnings of prayer

My first memory of praying was on my grandmother's knee. I have since learnt that grandmothers are often crucial in the religious lives of the young. She was a Wesleyan Methodist, whose standards of religious practice were shaped in the Westgate Methodist Chapel, in the Wear Valley, County Durham. When we went up to stay with her she would offer us barley sugars to go to sleep with, sugar cubes with tweezers for our tea, and a sugar shaker for our cornflakes. We loved all that, but there was an austerity too, with the wash tub and the mangle in the outhouse, no Sunday papers, and morning prayers in the dining-room. Being very young, I was put on her knee and we said prayers together. I cannot remember any words in particular, although there must have been some. I can only remember the physical sense of a plaid skirt and a well-laundered blouse, and a particularly cold piece of jewellery that used to stick in when the hugs became intense. Despite the brooch, it was a happy memory, and one which spoke to me of God. Prayer began for me informally, with someone else making up the prayers. At least, that is my earliest memory. A lot may have gone on before that with my parents, but the sense of being physically held in prayer was a very strong first experience.

I should imagine most early experiences of prayer are formed by a parent saying goodnight, and adding one or two prayers, and a 'God bless you'. It is unlikely to have been in church, or drawing on the riches of the Book of Common Prayer, but by another, warm, breathing, hopefully hugging, person combining love and prayer, with that warm proximity with which a shepherd might bring a lamb in from the cold at lambing time. It is unlikely to be a priest who does this, and I should think it more likely to be a woman than a man. Any extra prayers are most likely to consist of the Lord's Prayer, and the names of the family. More sophisticated families might add to this quite sufficient diet, thanksgivings and penitence, thank-yous and sorrys, and at its simplest it might just be 'Good night. God bless'.

Who knows how common this practice still is? I would not be surprised, even in this apparently godless age, if there were not still a great deal of this warm and comforting ritual practice at the bedside. It will take place throughout the world, in all sorts of languages, to all sorts of images of the godhead: as charms against the dark and the night, as a reinforcement of the parents' beliefs, or as a form of words handed on from generation to generation. For some it will never be so intense until the hours before they die, for others it will be a daily meeting with God.

The next memory after the prayers on the knee was a more solitary one. I remember taking a book of stories and pictures on the life of Christ to bed, and probably having them read to me. Then the book was left on the bed so I could stay awake that bit longer, and, alone, I stared at the picture of the crucifixion. The sky was a particularly dark blue colour and the white of Christ's loin-cloth stood out against it. I was struck dumb by this. My prayers dried up, and words were totally subsumed into the visual image. Instead of words, and the warmth of the grandmotherly embrace, I was left with intensity, a heightening of the emotions, myself alone, and the long night ahead. This was my introduction to solitary prayer, the struggling with the presence of God.

Prayer in church was yet another dimension, the appreciation of which came later still. Church memories are not essentially, or in the first place, memories of prayer, but rather a vague sense of smell, or light. When we went north to the land of Wesleyan Methodism it was the smell of the varnish on the pews, and even more vivid than the smell was the sight of the organist high up above the pulpit at the east end.

My image of the Holy Trinity was formed by this arrangement: God the organist at the top, Jesus the preacher in the middle, and the Holy Spirit was represented by a combination of the holy table, the flowers and the collection plate. The memory was warm and earnest, and there were some nice girls in the Sunday School.

At the other end of the country, which was more the haunt of my mother's family, was an Anglo-Catholic church in Folkestone. I was beached after falling ill with jaundice, in the hotel next door to the church. I could see the church through the window, and heard the bells on practice nights, but it wasn't until I was convalescing that I went inside the church to a service. I was so overwhelmed by the lights and the smell of incense that I cried, more with awe than with sadness, and had to come out.

The notion that a church had anything to do with praying came much later when I began to be interested in language, words, poetry and the service books themselves. I bought a copy of the English Missal from Mowbrays in Birmingham, with its services for Holy Week, its thin prayer-book paper, and, again, a picture of the crucified Christ. I discovered that prayer was actually words on a page as well as a voice from the front, and when the two matched, as they did occasionally in Holy Week or at the communion service, it satisfied a deep-seated need in me to have words and worship interlocking. What was being said reflected what was being done. Prayer, public prayer, took on the element of drama, and it began to work for me.

What I have been salvaging from my memory here are three fairly distinct areas of praying: public, private and something in between. The public area, in church, has a set form of words, which you can hopefully make your own by entering into their meaning and willing them to be true for you. In the private area, you wrestle like Jacob with the angel of God. Like Jesus in the Garden of Gethsemane you wrestle with your destiny, or like him you go secretly into the hills to pray. Then there is that area of praying which falls into neither of those fairly clearly defined previous two areas, but which begins with the informality of the bedside and the lap, and continues in the Christian life at moments when there is a strong sense that ordinary discourse, 'chat', has to give way to something different, something more elevated, or sacred, which is God-infused, God-directed and God-centred. It takes up our humanness, our predicaments, our cares and concerns, and offers them all up to God in prayer.

I am chancing the phrase 'pastoral prayer' here, as a way of defining it a little more clearly. As a clergyman, I have attended and led many services. I am expected to be proficient in those areas. We are encouraged throughout our ministry, by the example of Christ and by the wisdom of the spiritual teachers of the Church, and wider afield, to develop an interior life of prayer. What is less prepared for, and thought through, are those moments of prayer which sometimes are expected and sometimes just come upon us in company with others, in situations of pastoral care.

I am aware of the paradox here: how can we prepare for the spontaneous? The Spirit, you could say, blows where it will, not where you always want it to. Yet, with an increasing number of lay parishioners helping in the pastoral work of the Church, they will I am sure, be asking searching questions. For example, 'How can I prepare for those times when prayers will be expected of me?' 'What do I say?' 'When is it right to pray with another?' 'Where does the Holy Spirit fit into this?' 'Are there any good books on the subject, or wisdom to hand on?' 'What is the relationship between our private prayer, the public liturgy of the Church, and pastoral prayer?'

The area I have chosen to write about is largely a secret one. People are reticent, for many good reasons, about describing the events and emotions, and style of prayer, which they use in one-to-one visiting situations. As clergy, we may have done some joint visiting with our training incumbents and then discussed it, but from my own recollection, there wasn't a lot of that. We learnt on the job, and never quite knew if we were doing the right thing or not.

It would be fascinating to have seen George Herbert visiting his parishioners, and seen at first hand the way he mediated the love of God to them, or gone along into the houses of Salford in the 1930s with Canon Peter Green, or listened in to the confessional of the Curé d'Ars, but we can't. We can only surmise from what we know of their more public life, or from their writings or letters, or from reminiscences of parishioners.

I have talked to some priests in preparation for this book. There are those who find it very difficult indeed to pray with others, in an informal spontaneous way. They need the help of the more formal, but still private, orders of service for the sick, or express their pastoral care through a celebration, however brief, of the Holy Communion. Others find pastoral prayer quite natural, and are skilled in helping people grow in its practice. Canon Green said, 'Till you have got a man on his knees to pray, you have done nothing for him spiritually.' The underlying thought for me there is how good he probably was himself in helping others do just that. The question I have is, how did he manage it, and what can we learn from it?

I hesitated to go into the realms of questionnaires and interviews to gain vast amounts of material to come up with the perfect answer, because as I shall try and say later, one of the great things about prayer is that the self, the way you find it comfortable, will be the greatest guide. If you are doing what you find comfortable, it will no doubt convey itself to the other person. Confidence is catching.

If I convey a message of complete confidence myself, it would be misleading. I have struggled with this matter of praying with others, and often feel I should have done it when I did not. Strangely enough I have rarely felt it the other way round, that I should not have done when I did. That might be arrogance, or it might be saying something about the importance of prayer in the pastoral setting. None of us likes to be trapped into the situation of assisting someone else's escalating ego. Long and over-earnest prayers which are often little more than telling God what to do can be very off-putting. On the other hand, the inability to convey the sacred at moments of need can be a disappointment to someone who badly needs the word, the name, the assurance of sins forgiven or hope confirmed.

'Moments of Prayer' has been a working title for so long that it has stuck. I hope to convey the idea that prayer can never just be turned on at a moment's notice. Prayer is a life, a relationship between us, God and the other; a self-giving. There will be moments when this ongoing, underground existence of God will bubble up and make itself felt more strongly and vividly. It will crack through the surface in moments of transfiguration and meaning, in the moment of calling, and at the moment of forgiveness. These moments are rare, and come unexpectedly, when we are not looking, or forcing the pace, or demanding. God comes in his own moment.

This has not been written on a sabbatical. It has been squeezed into the daily routine of a parish priest, and many of the concerns which it expresses have arisen from my own time on the beat over the last twenty-five years. My Winchester parish is, in police terms, Beat 1. They have been years of intense activity, and always there has been a sense that more could have been done: more visiting, more time in preparation of sermons, more hours of prayer, more time with the family. I am sure I feel the same guilt that most clergy carry round with them.

There have been subtle shifts in the pressures over the years, and some good steps forward in thinking. On the good side, there seems to be a greater understanding of the problem of the endless agenda of care. Thoughtful spiritual directors usually point in the way of less activity rather than more. Over-activity, followed by burn-out or depression, or the breakdown of marriage relationships is an all too familiar picture. I think, I hope, more people are saying, your job as a priest is to pray, to study, to read, to be a still centre rather than a spinning wheel, to be wise for others, to keep a sense of humour, and to remain sane. So the priestly calling is preserved as one which keeps the channels open between God and the parish, and back from the parish to God.

However much we deflect leadership away from the parish

priest, in however big a parish or group of parishes, there will still be a very strong connection between leadership and the flavour, style, or atmosphere among the people. Charles de Foucauld, the French monk who inspired the founding of the Little Brothers and Sisters of Jesus, used to say, 'tel pasteur, tel peuple', 'as the pastor, so the people'. The longing for time for prayer is a longing to remain sane, and not to slide off into the vortex of activity or cynicism. The confidence of the clergy in themselves seems to have reached a pretty low ebb. The larder is looking empty, all the rations have been spent, and we look on a group of men and women, stretched to the limit, coping with prevailing ideologies in our society which are now so foreign to the source or root of the priestly life as understood in the Gospels.

The danger, and this is the bad side, is that we shall lose confidence in the inner voice which says the wellsprings of our life are in a loving, prayerful relation with God and with his people, and instead become administrators with no heart. The heart and the purpose will go out of the life. The parish priest's task has always been a heroic one. We do not match up to expectations, of course, but it was never meant to be safe. Our model is Christ himself who gave himself up for the sake of the world.

For Christ, that process of giving himself up, of assuming the nature of a slave, was a continual struggle which he handed over to his inner life of prayer, his imaginative life hid with God. The outward acts, or ministry of healing, casting out demons and raising the dead, were the outworkings of a life of prayer, of time spent with God, listening, sharing, deliberating.

How we do that prayer and listening in the context of our own places, with the bodies and souls we have been given and among the people who share our Christian lives, is the subject of this book. The minute particulars – the faces of the people, their tears and their laughter, their hats and their shoes, the weather, the view from the church door, the cakes they bake – all these add flavour to the prayer. Prayer is never sanitized, but rather full of the experiences of life lived with others, and if there is one thing that I really think I have failed with here, it is in giving the local flavour to the life of prayer. The glorious body that shall be will still in essence be the human body that was. If our prayer gets too holy and ceases to be grounded in the human, it is probably more of an ego-trip than a gathering up of the fragments of a particular place and an offering of them to God. How prayer, in a more particular sense, is affected by the human and natural landscape, rather than just by a direct relationship with God, is something that I have not worked out at any depth, but if we pray for and with people, and those people are rooted in a landscape, then that landscape will affect the prayer. Jesus' eye was often for the landscape and the inner weather of people: he spotted the corn and the darnel, the lost coin, the first signs of summer; he knew the importunate widow, the Good Samaritan, the housekeeper, the bridegroom. They were part of his parish, as they are a part of ours. He saw through them to the signs of the Kingdom. The sacramental or expressive nature of all things is one of the greatest stimulae to prayer. It is just that our society, our world, loses touch with the springs of the natural world, 'nor can foot feel being shod', and the prayer, rather than being enriched by the particular, becomes a plea to discover the true particular, the true identity of people in Christ.

Preparation and prayer

So you pray to learn how to pray.
Thomas Merton

———

And now let's tune our instruments.
George Herbert

1

Preparation and prayer

i Desiring God

Walking round Winchester I am constantly surprised and
enchanted by the sudden appearance, in all sorts of places, of
clear, running water. It is clear because it runs over chalk, and
its sudden appearances are largely due to the arrangement,
back in Anglo-Saxon days, of the water courses through the
town. They are much built over now, and so it is even more
remarkable when they appear. They really are 'streams of living
water'.

When King Alfred, who knew Winchester well, was translating one of the most important books on the pastoral life of
the clergy, Pope Gregory's *Pastoral Rule*, he could not resist
writing his own preface to it in verse. The poem takes the
image of the streams running through Winchester and compares them to the inspiration flowing out from the Holy
Spirit into and through the channels provided by the people
of God. Those people, us if you like, need to make ourselves
available as channels or conduits for this Spirit to flow. Prayer,
as the power of God at work, flows similarly. It is an intensely
woven poem, which, if unpicked, could give us many
thoughts, but as we think about the way we approach prayer,
or understand it working in us and for us, Alfred has this to
say:

> These are the waterscapes that God has promised
> as a comfort to the world.
> He said that he would wish for evermore
> that living waters should flow into the world,

11

from the hearts of all, beneath the sky,
that faithfully believe in him. There is little doubt
these waterscapes their wellspring have
in heaven, that is the Holy Ghost.
From which the saints, and chosen ones, can draw.

This word picture on the source of prayer kindles our imaginations. We cannot assume that prayer just happens. It is a life, a relationship, a sending and a receiving, a longing and a providing. It is often difficult to distinguish prayer from life.

You cannot turn on prayer like a tap and expect anything to come out of it if there has been no connecting up of the tap with the main supply. Day after day we have to maintain that connection with the source of prayer, which is the Holy Spirit of God. That is not to say that if, after long years of neglect, we turn back to the source in heartfelt prayer the supply will not be instantly available, but the will to turn to God gets weaker and weaker, and the will in prayer is all important. Will is rather a cold word; we associate it with 'iron' and Victorian public schools, but it has an important place in the vocabulary of prayer, as the strength with which we commit ourselves to the love of God.

Desire is perhaps a better word. We have to desire God to begin in prayer. There has to be some sort of spark within us which begins that process, which the Holy Spirit can then fan into flame. The very beginning of prayer is a joining of desires, and like human love it is a great mystery how attraction begins. We can only search into our own hearts to see how that miracle was wrought in our own lives. We can uncover the means by which prayer, which is the desire to be with God, took hold of our lives. Prayer is a process of communing: it is best held in a total relation, with all that we do and all that we are, gently, through life. I say gently because to snatch for it is often to miss it. Baron von Hügel, a well-known spiritual writer and director of souls, said in a letter to his niece, 'Even if dying, never strain'. In the same way Jesus did not grasp or clutch at equality with God, but proceeded with humility, and a gentle emptying of himself, so that the divine within could be revealed (Philippians 2.6–11).

Our desire is not just revealed in an outpouring of words, it is a relationship of love, of caring, of belonging. Words are one way of expressing this deep subterranean longing, but without the desire there would be nothing for the words to express. So beneath the language of prayer lies a secret and silent area of being in relation with God. This is a very hard thing to convey or to communicate to someone else, but it is fundamental to our understanding of prayer.

What do I mean by 'being in relation with God'? How does it affect us in a practical way, and how can we tell whether prayer and life are coming together? There is a brief saying of Jesus which gives us a clue. Jesus said, it's no good just saying 'Lord, Lord' and expecting to be saved; instead we have to do the will of our heavenly Father. Prayer does not work from the lips outwards, but from the heart, and the heart not as something merely emotional but as something which is given strength and structure by our will, or our desire. So the secret working of our heart has its test in the way we work things out in the ordinary course of everyday living, from which none of us are exempt. If the cry 'Lord, Lord!' is merely empty sounds then it misses the gospel command to do the will of our heavenly Father. What that will is, has to be sought, found and incorporated into our daily lives.

At the beginning, this sorting out what exactly is the will of God might seem a bit laborious, simple and self-conscious. You might have to make up your mind whether it is better to have a quarter of an hour reading a chapter of the Bible than a quarter of an hour reading the newspaper. At the beginning there is a tussle. You might, after much heart-searching decide that God would want you to know what is happening in the world in order to pray better, but it is also important to read the Scriptures. So, what is the will of God in that instance? After a pause for reflection you decide to spend half the time reading the Scriptures and half the time reading the newspaper. In time, if we stay self-critical in the presence of God we shall find out whether this decision was right. What

13

at first was a long-winded decision process becomes easier, more automatic, and in more and more aspects of our life we are able to do the will of our heavenly Father.

To do the right thing, and to sort out in our consciences what is the right thing, we need time for reflection. To persevere in this process of evaluating the will of God there must be some desire to do it; and we get back to the spark of desire fanned into flame by the Holy Spirit. Before all the doing, there needs to be an orientation, a thrust, an urgency of longing, which is at the centre of our being. We need, to put it simply, to love God.

The distinction between being and doing is one that often is mentioned in this context. It can get a bit philosophical to distinguish between those two words. The gospel distinction is the one that Jesus draws between Martha and Mary. Mary represents the contemplative 'being' side of our nature, and Mary the 'doing' side. The gospel makes a crucial judgement between the two and comes down on the side of Mary, who had discovered the secret that there is only one thing necessary, to sit at the feet of Christ and to gaze upon his face. I think I can now just about tell the difference, even if I cannot put it into practice very well.

I can just about feel when I am at the disposal of God in prayer and when I am not. When I am, I am consciously focused on the desire to be with God. There is a stillness, a silence, and an expectancy in myself, which has none of the nervousness of waiting for a human guest, but is a real peace.

This process of being can begin with a piece of religious music, or a paragraph from a spiritual writer, or a line or two from Scripture, but it is very passive, calm, peaceful and deeply satisfying. Unlike Gethsemane, you could say. There are Gethsemane times, but, if we look carefully, Christ found through the Gethsemane experience that strength and peace of commitment when he handed over his will to God. It is this which builds up our being with God, so that when the alarm bells ring and we rush off to visit a dying person, or the parents of a young man killed on the farm, or the wife of a middle-aged man who has died of a heart attack, we are ready. God, desired in the conscious decisions of our daily life, is there when we make the automatic actions and decisions. The channels have been maintained, the water of the Spirit runs freely.

That sounds easy, and I am conscious that I have made it sound too automatic: 'If x, then y; if we love God then everything will run smoothly when it comes to pastoral work.' I know that that is not quite right, and my colleagues in far more difficult circumstances certainly do not find it that easy. 'What about when I open my mouth and nothing comes out?' 'What about when I feel like saying, O God, this is awful'? Can our response to situations ever be really adequate?

There are times when we are dumbfounded. As dumbfounded as the people we are trying to pray with and minister to. To share in that sense of loss and failure with others must be right, but how we convey the love of God and support others in those situations will need to rest on our homework in prayer. I feel the wise path would be to translate our grief or anger or sense of shock into a language which the others can manage and handle without increasing their own pain or fear. Through experience we learn appropriate responses. It may happen that, later on, on our own, the sorrow we have felt will be allowed its natural response. In discussing this with others, most have confessed to needing times to go away and howl.

Coping with the many difficulties that occur when we begin to want to pray, and that means when we start in the course of our life, as well as every time we set out to pray during the day, is something that persists. Dealing with something so intangible there are bound to be problems of getting into prayer: wondering if I am doing the right thing, distractions, a downright sense of irrelevance, a real heartache at the apparent absence of God.

We long for more reassurance, good marks, stars on the chart, badges, medals even, for perseverance, but no, just a strange unworldly silence. Slowly, that lack of anything positive in a worldly sense begins to have a more profoundly satisfying outcome or feeling. We move from one stage into another, closer to the God who is longing for us to get free from the customary rewards for human activity into 'another country'. By all accounts, this transference, or journey, has been experienced by many, and variously described as going through a dark night or as a desert period, in which God is turning us inside out, stripping us of all our customary treats and rewards. The cloud is another picture of this experience in which we see little of the way ahead but we live by faith, and we live and feed on the love that sets us off in the first place. God touches us with his hand, our heart responds with such fullness and eagerness, and then begins the unlearning, the painful removal of self-will, our old identity. Prayer is God remaking us, back into our original image.

In practice that means a lot of drab times, illuminated by Scripture and the stories of the saints who have gone along the same road. It is also illuminated by those who are struggling and suffering in ways other than the spiritual. We can easily get too inward-looking and self-centred. Only when we meet with people who are being challenged in deep ways do we begin to forget ourselves and go out to others in love. So we manage the process by fulfilling the second commandment; the love of God and the love of our neighbour, as St John knew and wrote about in his letters, are intimately entwined. Caring about others really enriches the life of prayer, because it is doing God's will without an undue concern for self.

ii Silent adoration

In some ways, prayer is always a preparation. We are always preparing to be with God in this life. The fullness of God in Christ is realized, but not yet fully experienced. Our preparation for pastoral prayer is all important. Our lives do not naturally stop to give us pause for reflection. They rush on headlong, with ever-increasing busyness. That means we have to plan to stop, to put it into our personal and our parish diaries to stop. The Church gives us Lent and Advent to do a bit of 'loitering with intent', but we tend to fill those up too. Each day we need a time to pause and be available to God, without a particular agenda if possible, except to be with God and to offer our hearts for refreshing at his spring. Each year we need a longer time, a retreat, a serious commitment to put behind us our worldly agenda and offer ourselves to God for renewal. On a three-day retreat we can spend one day winding down, one day of real resting in the presence of God, and another half day seeing what practical things we can do to let God have more say in our daily life.

This space Christ found in his ministry during his nights of prayer and in his rests in Bethany before the days of intense activity in Jerusalem. He made time in the wilderness before the major period of ministry to the sick, the dying and the spiritually hungry and thirsty.

Jesus asked his disciples to watch for the coming of the Kingdom. We could understand the Kingdom to be the specific call on our time to be ministering to the needs of others. The Kingdom we were watching and waiting for in the silence becomes the Kingdom within us and around us in the Casualty Ward, in the homes of people and as we meet them in the street.

Prayer is not just word-shaped, it is life-shaped, and words can sound very empty indeed if they do not proceed from a life lived with God. Our words and our life must be of a piece. Our inside has to match our outside to escape the accusation of hypocrisy. If our words and our lives are not of a piece, then there will be a hollow ring to them. The words of the Lord's Prayer, 'Thy will be done', remind us of our commitment to live out what we have discovered of the love of God in our prayers. In this sense, doing feeds being, and Martha and Mary become complementary figures. Our visiting will feed our prayers and our prayers will nourish our visiting.

Before any public activity of prayer there must have been some growing going on. Think of the seed growing in the dark, secret, silent earth. That is where the true organic, authentic life begins, and what is true for biological life is also true for the spiritual life. Our knowing God, and being known of him, takes place in the dark and secret place of growth, in the country of silence and of no words. That room we are bidden to return to by Christ is where we shut the door and pray to the Father who sees in secret.

Going into a room is quite a practical, bodily thing to do. Prayer is not always just a completely spiritual thing. We are bodies as well as souls, and our bodies can assist our prayer as much as they can distract. We just have to get them to work for us. Our prayer needs grounding. We need to find a place on the face of the earth where we can do our praying. A place where we stop the business of life and encounter the living God. The daily bread of the Lord's Prayer needs a place to rise and an oven to be baked in. Prayer too has its very practical side, and for me that means quite a lot of 'nots': not walking around fidgeting, not looking for a book, not dreaming of what my room might look like with a bit of rearrangement. I have to be firm with the 'nots' before the 'yeses' begin. The yeses begin with 'Yes, I do want to sense the closeness of the presence of Christ, and yes I must calm down and regulate my breathing so that I can sense the great gift of life coming from its source in the creator God, and yes I will leave the page of my heart blank for Christ to write his wisdom on.'

All this goes on, day by day, building up a life lived with God, absorbing his word in Scripture, his art and sculpture in creation, his drama in the seasons and their weather, his humanness in Jesus, his irresistibility in the Holy Spirit. All this goes on before a word is spoken. Without that silent preparation, a word will fail to have its power. Anyone working with a craft will tell you of the hours of silent struggle, the failed attempts, the groans, the sighs, the lack of applause which accompany the process of creativity.

So it is with pastoral prayer. It must emanate from a life of prayer. A life rooted in the great mystery of Christ, which, as we go deeper, opens out into the greater mystery of the one in three. We discover that the Spirit which moves us to pray, moves us closer to Christ, and the closer to Christ that we live, the closer to God, who in turn offers himself to us in the human form of Jesus. This trinitarian air we breathe in prayer is circulating in a wide and welcoming room. It is evidence that we never pray out of our own resources; we pray in the presence and power of God, Father, Son and Holy Spirit.

If this sounds rarified to you then I apologise. I am only charting a journey I have tried to go along myself, and therefore, because of its essential intimacy, might seem strange. But the point I want to make is that unless you have some sort of private, intimate relationship with God, it is unlikely that what you say in a pastoral relationship will have authenticity. The model is Jesus himself. He spoke with authority; the authority of one who was on intimate terms with God, his Father. We aim for that. We fall terribly short. We send off arrows from all sorts of different places, but their target is a common one, to desire God.

There are a great deal of resources to help us here. Many people have written down the account of their relationship with God. We can catch from them something of the feel of it and much of the route they have taken: St Theresa of Avila's *Life*, St Augustine's *Confessions*, John Henry Newman's *Apologia*, Mother Julian's *Revelations*, Thomas Traherne's *Centuries*. Each is a very different story, differently told, but in each case we have a good example of that inward voyage. The value of a book in which you share the spiritual experiences of others can be very great. Suggesting a book is a difficult thing, because you never quite know if it is the right book at the right time for someone. An element of the miraculous or the providential often comes into it. Browsing along the shelves of the public library under religion, I picked out a book which had a picture on the cover. The picture was of a monk standing in a forest, and the title was *Thoughts in Solitude*. I had never heard of Thomas Merton, the author, before, but the photograph led me into other books by Merton, and into the whole world of contemplative spirituality. It was the summer of 1965 and they were the heady days of taking the book into the churchyard near the library and reading great chunks of spirituality, of which I understood not a word, but subconsciously was responding to the

19

language of prayer. My heart pounded with a love for solitude in which I could be with God, as much as it pounded with 60s music, and leapt around uncontrollably for human love. The book was a way of being with another, without the distraction of a bodily presence. It was a meeting of souls.

iii Prayer and Scripture

> Will you be diligent in Prayers, and in reading of the holy Scriptures, and in such studies as help to the knowledge of the same, laying aside the study of the world and the flesh?
>
> I will endeavour myself so to do, the Lord being my helper.
> (*The Anglican Ordinal*)

This admonition in the ordination service is a timely reminder of the importance to all our work of the reading of the holy Scriptures. We often have to take it on trust that this reading does filter through into our lives as ministers and pastors. The effects are often hidden to us, while they might be glaringly obvious to others. We cannot keep taking the lid off the pot to see how we are working inside, but from much of the wisdom handed on we trust that keeping close to Scripture in our reading, thinking and praying we shall be shaped and formed in a helpful way. Because that formation has been such a stormy ride for me, I offer my own journey as a guide to seeing some of the joys and sorrows that lie between first confronting Scripture and using it, and being used by it, to convey its truth to others in life.

My relationship with the writings of 'long ago', or 'the things written aforetime' (Romans 15.4) has been a long one, and an up-and-down one. It has gone through phases which I can now see for what they were, and I can also see how different they were from each other. It began with the consciousness of a book. Here was a special artefact which was physically different from most of the books I had read to me, or owned. The writing was in four columns and was printed on specially thin paper, and the idea that it had any relation to the stories I had been told was purely one of trust. I knew that stories came from books, and so here was the book that those stories came from, and that was that. I looked at the book and turned the pages in a state of mysterious awe. Only slowly, as I learned to read, did the cramped print begin to match up to the stories I had been told. The mental images that I had, of the road to Jericho for example, were not changed greatly by the words. The words had to fit into my prearranged mental images. There is no shimmering heat described in St Luke's parable of the Good Samaritan, but my imagination put it there, and there it stayed.

As I got to know the words of the Authorized Version of the Bible, so I realized that here, between the covers, were not just stories. Here were other sorts of words which related to some inner feelings, to states of being: 'enmity' was being angry with another. I knew that one because I had to read it at the Carol Service, and the smallest and the youngest boy always had to struggle with the 'Fall of Man' from Genesis 3. 'Charity', on the other hand, was the opposite state, of being friendly or in harmony. 'Vanity', the great word which one of our preachers boomed out to us, I understood to mean useless or nothingness, not just preening yourself in front of the mirror. On the one hand I had a store of images deriving from the narratives, and on the other hand a set of emotional labels: the one largely to do with Jesus, and the Old Testament, and the other, seemingly, to do with Paul.

That duality, a childlike love of stories, preferably with pictures, and a growing involvement with the abstract map of ideas and states of being, saw me through my teens. A university course in theology made things no clearer. Drowning in a sea of complexity, and feeling I had to know everything about everything in a hurry, complicated things and distanced me from the text. An over-developed curiosity in the sources that lay behind them prevented me from the simple joys of reading the stories at their face value. Too conscientious to sort the wheat from the chaff, and too dense to

21

put everything together in an ordered shape, I left with an actor's degree and with my free copies of the Hebrew Bible and the Greek New Testament.

Of course, things had been going on underground of which I was not aware at the time. The classes in Hebrew and Greek gave me the smattering of knowledge I needed to take a deeper interest in the words. The sensitivity to the idea of source material edited by each of the gospel writers gave me, in time, a great sympathy with the authorship process and with the authors themselves. I admired the struggle, the craftsmanship, the creativity of ordering the borrowed material. I was right in there, in the workshop, with them. Too worldly wise now for the stories as stories, and too simple-minded for the arguments and controversies that clogged the Epistles of Paul, I turned to secular literature – novels, plays, poetry – which spoke of a world I knew about and lived in. The Scriptures, 'the Bible', seemed like some intellectual aunt whom I visited out of a sense of duty from time to time, who I knew was worthy and intelligent but who slightly reached out the hand of death in welcome. Basically, I did not know the Bible well enough, did not handle it daily, did not know its weight or feel, and rather set it over against myself.

I was making these discoveries at a time in history when the Bible was suffering from one great disadvantage. The problem that my generation has had with regard to the Scriptures is the lack of a generally recognized authorized text. We have been through many different translations: NEB, RSV, JB, REB, NRSV. The language has not stuck and does not reverberate with the world around it. There is no bouncing back of language from the talk we have in the sitting-room to the words we hear on Sunday or read during the week. The Scriptures are becoming beleaguered, with no wider cultural reference and no great interest in their content, so the Bible lies around the house rather like *The Book of the Dead* did in my childhood. We can no longer take for granted, in the times we spend together as Christians, that the unspoken groundwork will be biblical, and the language in

22

which we talk about the things of God will be a common parlance.

There is a diffuseness in our lectionaries, our Bible translations and in our approach to the Bible. It is a case of everyone for themselves, and lucky the person who finds a teacher or a guide who can provide any footholds to Scripture which make it more than just entertainment, as in the rock musical *Joseph and His Technicolour Dreamcoat*, or billboard clichés like 'The End of the World is Nigh!'

Despite all the downs, I am beginning to discover the glory and excitement of Scripture in its translucent, sacramental quality. Like Josiah discovering the old book of the Law which had been hidden away in a dusty cupboard in the Temple, I am beginning to read the words and hear them as if for the first time. More often than not I am transported by them into another world, another atmosphere. I am able to pass through the everyday letters and syllables into something else, something other. The more we make the Scriptures our own, the more we sense the internal echoes and mutuality of the writings, and the more they settle into a pattern which inhabits not just our minds or hearts, but our whole being, the more they resonate for us. I know there are awful bits, and wrong bits, repeated bits and cruel bits, and I do not believe every word to be true in exactly the same way. The more I experience life with all its horrors and wars, and violent deaths and cruelty, as well as its great beauty and heart-lurching generosity of spirit, so does my love of the Scriptures as a source of fresh and living water match up with that. And as I reflect on how that change has come about since the end of college days I have to put it down to at least three things.

Getting back behind the very strong influence of the 'scientific' criticism of the Bible which has been dominant for the last two hundred years, and entering the pre-Enlightenment world of commentators like Augustine, John Chrysostom and Bede, has helped me have a more soul-orientated or poetic approach to reading and using the Bible. For these

23

people, words and phrases are allowed to roam hither and thither around both their minds and the Bible itself, regardless of their historical order. By a poetic approach, I mean the range of response we can give to words like bread, water, fire or garden, and to sense the way in which the writers are building on the insights of others and trying to maintain a unity within the multi-coloured whole. It is to understand that their greatest concern was not always historical accuracy as we understand that now, but to make the hidden secrets of God luminous to our believing and trusting souls.

The particular books of the Bible which hold a central pivotal position, actually and metaphorically, and which have particularly resonated with me through this period are the Psalms, the Song of Songs, and the Gospel of St Mark. The Psalms have always been seen as the prayer book of the Bible, and it should come as no surprise that to one interested in poetry these are particularly accessible. With all their presentation of the ups and downs in the experience of loving God, and with their rich use of images and their joy in language, they provide the backbone of the Church's daily prayer and have been the source of its meditation. They were that for Jesus, too. Thomas Merton, the poet and Trappist monk, wrote, 'Meditation on the psalms, inspired by love, is the key to the mystery of the divine compassion.'

The Song of Songs seems to me a book for those who are eager to relate the human emotion of love to the work and purposes of God. It is blatantly a love poem. It revels in the glories of the body, in bodies together, and in the relationship of love that makes such physicality meaningful and glorious. It speaks the language of desire. I have spent a long time with this book, translating it from the Hebrew, reading different translations and reading some of the medieval commentaries that supported the flowering of the mystical life in the Middle Ages. It has increased my sensitivity to the beauty of human, physical love. I do not now only have to love the sight of fields of ripe corn and dawns and dusks, I can relish a peopled landscape too. It helps us to say positive things about marriage in the Christian tradition. Coming where it does in the middle of the Old Testament as we have it, it almost physically generates excitement for God before it and after it. It humanizes the collection and it exalts it. As I come to see the body and soul as intimately entwined, its allegorization as a story of the love of God by his beloved is not a deviation but another level of meaning which assists the life of prayer. God is as beautiful as the most beautiful person in the world. How privileged and with what delight do we sit near him, as St John sat next to Christ at the Last Supper, and talk with him and listen to him. The adolescent fixations have to be worked through, both with people and with our idea of God, and that can be a painful process, but the Song of Songs leads us on into maturity and does not desert us just because we are growing up. Like the image of the garden, which the song sets centrally in its own text, we have seasons too. To read the commentaries on the Song by John of the Cross and by Theresa of Avila, or to see how John Keble regarded it, or Bernard of Clairvaux, or George Herbert in his poem 'Love', or Gregory of Nyssa, or St John the Evangelist, or Thérèse of Lisieux, we get a growing concourse of people who have not jettisoned desire as the basic mainspring of their love of God, but who have transfigured desire and made it holy by allowing God to re-create it in them.

St Mark's Gospel has helped me particularly because I see in it, more clearly than in the others, the hand of a writer under duress. It has also for my generation been considered to be the earliest of the Gospels, and the one on which the others were in some senses based. The Gospel shows the stress of the time, of the political dangers in Rome, and the struggle of the writer to be an adequate channel of the truth as he received it and experienced it. Each book of the Bible carries its own excitement of discovering what is being said and how it is saying it. St Mark stayed with me through the up-and-down years, and helped me to keep praying. That is not to say that St John's sweeping vistas of eternity and the intensity of the love of God have not helped. On the contrary, there are times when, as John sat with Christ at the Last Supper, so I have wanted to sit with St John, but Mark's stripped urgency for faith has kept me rooted to the point where the cross meets the soil. Mark also keeps the pressure on me to decide, and to keep deciding urgently. He helps me to make each day one that can be open to either hearing or not hearing, seeing or being obstinately blind, believing and trusting or being afraid. When it comes to being with people in a pastoral situation or on the edge of prayer, Mark helps me to feel an urgent longing to share with them a need to submit to faith in Christ, at the same time as being aware of the difficulties of that. Mark's Gospel, and the Christ portrayed in his Gospel, goes on that path too.

Another thing that has brought a relish to my reading of the Bible is the use of a time after it, and sometimes, if the occasion is fitting, during it – to stop, pause, think, mull over what I have just read. When I was a curate I used to go for long stomps with a neighbouring curate. He would always heave a sigh of relief when his vicar went on holiday, because it meant that he could take the daily office at his own pace, which I am sure would have been slower and more reflective than the racing demon pace of his vicar. I discovered the joy of giving space to words so that they had time to go and come back with their creative echoes. I did not just treat the Bible as a series of stories which had an ending I had to get to, and the sooner the better, but as seeds which dropped into my soul, one by one, and I allowed them to grow within me. The Parable of the Sower (Mark 4) is about Scripture dropping into us, into the rich and fertile soil of a listening, receiving soul. That process simply cannot be rushed. More time is being set aside in public worship now for reflective listening, and the influence of the Taizé community's custom of silence in their prayer time has helped us see it as important and enjoyable. So that instead of being fearful of silence, we begin to want longer and longer stretches of it.

The prayerful reading of Scripture in our own homes is perhaps nothing new to those who have been following a series of Bible reading notes, and are used to the habit of reading with a time of reflection added to it. To others, it may be new, and they wait for permission to dream dreams during

Bible reading and to follow the leads that their imagination sets off. 'Imagination' is the key word here. It is the playful part of the mind which links up the outer and the inner worlds, the story and the emotions or the abstract ideas, which we were talking about before. The imagination should be the lively centre of seeing possibilities and of processing information to make it part of ourselves. So the Bible contains many pictures of how things could and should be, and we need a place to process that material and to do something with it. What does it mean for me? What links does it have with my experience? How does it tie up with other things I have read or felt?

S. T. Coleridge (1772–1834), the poet and religious philosopher, talked about the difference between 'fantasy' and 'imagination', and I think it is a helpful distinction to draw with our approach to Bible reading. Fantasy takes images and excites the mind in ways so removed from reality that it builds up a frustration and anxiety when they are not realized. The imagination, Coleridge said, is the creative thought process which is able to transform pictures and images into realistic routes for charting a way forward. Again, the art analogy helps. The artist takes material that is reasonably familiar to most people and makes new, unique patterns out of it. That creative process can be used with our reading of Scripture. The building bricks of Scripture are reasonably familiar, but our imaginations can reassemble them in unique ways in order to let God speak and act through us for our time. Prayer assists that releasing of the imaginative encounter with the texts, but because it gives time and space for the imagination to work, it checks the onrush of fantasy, and it channels the gift of the Holy Spirit, which is the power to act and the wisdom to guide. To give time for that process to work within us is invaluable for our reflecting on passages of Scripture. We keep the words, as Mary did, pondering them in our hearts, reliving the deep experiences, and as we do that we 'feel the finger of God and find it', and find Christ too. Christ provides that unitive vision as he stands at the mountain top beckoning all truth.

27

iv Putting it into words

The eighteenth-century musician Johann Joachim Quantz wrote a classic book about the flute and composed some wonderful music for that instrument. With that book in mind, the twentieth-century poet, W. S. Graham, wrote a series of six poems charting the progress of a teacher leading his pupil through the painful process of learning to play the flute. It is a splendid sequence, and most helpful in charting progress in the spiritual life. All six poems are about preparation. There is the long, hard, cold slog of getting your instrument to do what you want it to do, and of being in harmony with it and with the music. So it is with us in our preparations for those single, crucial moments when we are asked to mediate the love of God through ourselves, our instruments. Those moments when all the experiences we have had, the teaching, reading, talking, listening come to a head, and when we simply slip away and let the music, or in our case the Holy Spirit, take over.

When it eventually comes to putting our thoughts and feelings about God into words, if the practice has been done, then one of two things will occur. If the heart is in the right place then, in some ways, it does not matter what you say, because the words will speak with their own authority, or they spill out from a life lived with God. Having helped the seed develop within, the shoot and the flower follow naturally. We shall be in Christ, and Christ the Word will speak in us, and for us. We simply let him do the work and try not to get in the way. If we are practiced in the spiritual life, then we learn to be invisible and let the Holy Spirit speak through us, but the all too human side of our life blocks and darkens the clarity and light of Christ.

It is because of this blocking that penitence should take such an important part in our private prayer. This involves a continual awareness of the adequacy of Christ, and the inadequacy of ourselves, an awareness of the limitations of our words and the waywardness of our tongues, keeping a check on our faults, humility in confessing them, and seeking for forgiveness. Put like that in a world of sophisticated counselling methods, psychiatrists' couches and character assessment, it all seems rather amateur, but the simple barefoot doctor method of penitence, saying sorry to God, might be a much simpler and much cheaper route to wholeness of life. It is not our words but Christ the Word behind all we say that is the aim. That does not make us Christ, far from it; we simply allow ourselves to be instruments of God's word in particular human situations.

We are the human filter or channel through which God wills to speak in the local situation. We are not angels, we are human, and the call to minister is a call in a specific place at a particular time. There are the local conditions, and so if we try to be invisible ciphers of Christ's word, we may find that has to be translated into a language which the listener will understand. Here lies the challenge. It would be easy if we could just press a 'Christ button' and out come the right words for the right occasion, but it is not like that. Christ gives us the heart and the mind to communicate his word, and the final ingredient is the risk and the skill to speak that word in a way that will be heard and understood. At this point we should tremble, for this is the whole area of empathy and 'knowing the scene' and listening before speaking. All that can be learnt in time, but to get the right direction and strength to begin with is what our life of prayer is all about. Will to get that right, desire to know and love God in the face of Jesus Christ, and the way is clear to know, love and assist those we serve.

You can pray with them sometimes, but pray for them always.

Geoffrey Studdert-Kennedy

———

There was a part of the parish that few knew.

R. S. Thomas

2

Prayer and visiting

i Preparing to go

One of the most unlikely stories about prayer combined with deciding in which direction to go comes to us from *The Little Flowers of St Francis*. I set it at the head of this chapter to remind us partly of the folly of God (1 Corinthians 1.25), and partly to set the context of decision-making, which usually seems such a grown-up and serious thing, in the context of the Holy Spirit, where it seems rightly to belong. To depend entirely on our own wisdom in decisions is certainly a weighty and serious matter, but to remember that all things, in the end, rest on the providence of God is to lighten our burden considerably. The echoes of Mother Julian's phrase 'All shall be well, and all manner of thing shall be well' ring round the heavy atmosphere of board-rooms and synods, with their outrageous and bracing optimism.

St Francis and his friend Brother Masseo, so the story goes, were travelling along a road and they came to a three-way junction: one went to Siena, one to Florence and one to Arezzo. 'Which way shall we go?' asked the troubled Masseo. 'The road that God wants us to take,' said St Francis. 'But how are we to learn God's will?' asked Brother Masseo. Then Francis asked Masseo to spin round faster and faster, and when he said stop, then in whichever way Masseo was pointing they would go. After a considerable time, Francis said 'Stop!' and Masseo tumbled in the direction of Siena. So Siena it was. Masseo was bemused, giddy and annoyed, and wondered, like any self-respecting person might, what Francis was thinking about. It was only when they both got to Siena, at the same time as an internecine brawl was going on that Masseo realized the benefits of this seemingly random decision. Francis 'spoke to the men involved in this brawl with such devotion and holiness that he reconciled them to one another in complete unity, peace, and friendship'. The end, you might say, justified the means, and the wisdom we understand from all this is to allow God to make the decision, in whatever way he wants.

Having said that the first and primary aim of prayer is to be in relation with God, we move on to see how that relationship affects our decision-making. It is the point at which prayer seeks to come out of the closet of silence and contemplation, and move us, armed with wisdom and the Spirit of God, into the real world. For the pastor, that means searching out the sick, the troubled and those needing support in the journey of their faith.

I think we could call St Francis' way the 'whirling dervish' approach to decision-making. I now want to describe what you might call the 'Hollywood' approach. The difference between this and the previous dramatics is that rather than relying on God's providence, you act out the externals of what you think it might be like to be totally at the will of God, rather than living a whole life under God's direction. Trust has to begin from the heart, rather than from the outside gesture. In a moment of extreme emotional crisis you fall on the ground and lay yourself completely at the mercy of God for an answer, a miracle, a personal appearance of the Messiah. I can remember with embarrassment trying this myself. It seemed to be the only way out, but the answer did not come; there was no miracle and no appearance. Over the next few months life took on a different and a clearer shape, and the adolescent desperation turned into a realization that I was being rather self-centred, unrealistic and over-romantic. It was the only thing I could have done at the time, and it did bear some resemblance to the Gethsemane experience, but I am now not surprised that the answer did not come immediately, because patience was built into God's response.

Patience was what I needed to learn. Miracles are rare. More often than not we come to understand things better in the real situations of ordinary life, and not in self-dramatized scenarios of 'Hollywood' prayer.

More likely to yield fruitful decisions are the times of recollection, 'in the presence of God', when issues will appear, rise to the surface of our minds and appeal for consideration. Take, for example, the problem of who, among the many thousands of people who could be visited, we do in fact choose. You may be a systems person, and you only have to press the right buttons on your computer and it tells you who to visit, and very efficient it is too. Anniversaries of baptisms and bereavements, one month, three months, six months, are laid out before you. St Francis, and I suppose the more intuitive among us, would take a different course.

You might take this problem of who to visit. It needs a decision. You carry the question into your time of prayer and laying the parish before God in the cinema of your soul, you ask for a way forward to be made clear, the block of fear or ignorance to be removed. Give the issue time to come into focus. Wait patiently for the preliminary adverts and trailers of forthcoming films to finish. It may be that nothing directly to do with the actual question on your mind strikes you, but something completely different, a vision or a fresh understanding of some great religious truth is revealed. A picture from the Gospels comes to you and sets your difficulty in the context of a wider faith. The picture of Christ on the cross gives you a renewed vision that this was the one who cared about people, who went out to them, at the cost of his own security, reputation and health, and is also the one who comes out to you. This draws you out from the particular concern for individuals into the orbit of God's love, and there you might be happy to stay for a while.

You still need someone to visit, so you continue without anxiety, having placed the problem in God's care. Faces and names swim to the surface, and one by one we can commend them to God. Some people actually like to take in their address book to the time of prayer, or to a prayer vigil, and without doubt God will prompt you. He will give you someone who needs you – probably someone who had been on your conscience for some time, but who needed to come into focus.

When it comes to preparing to visit, we need to make a conscious decision to visit. A visit that is born out of prayer can never really be just a social visit. You lay it before God for his blessing, help and inspiration. God is always with us, but as we visit in his name we carry that extra charge, to leave the person better, closer to God than before we visited. That is nothing we can do on our own behalf, except by our desire or our intention. 'When you go into a house, let your first words be, "Peace to this house." If there is a man of peace there, your peace will rest on him.' (Luke 10.5–6). In the gospel command, there is a sense that every crossing of the threshold is a sacred act.

Prayer helps define the visits that are particularly 'spiritual' visits, so it is important not to go with too much of our own agenda, if any, because there is a real need to be met in the other. With visiting there is the problem of self-indulgence, and even visiting with the purpose of eyeing the antiques or satisfying one's own emotional needs. Prayer sorts this out. What are your motives for going? Most frequently it is to meet an obvious need – baptism, bereavement, sickness, an enquiry about church, new members of the parish – and to set those in the context of prayer. A conscious act of prayer before setting out is helpful. Occasionally, when we are entering unknown and sometimes dangerous areas, then the armour of God, which is prayer, is even more important! 'Be on your way; I am sending you like lambs among wolves' (Luke 10.3).

Some people will have their visiting very well organized, on a regular routine basis. Computers are now in use for assisting clergy and lay people alike in the timing of visits and the storing of information. Others will be random, and most will be somewhere in between. To commend the venture to God, whatever system or non-system you have, will allow

God to work more creatively in the situation. But the mysterious welling-up within, the call to go out and be with someone in the presence of God, is the adventure we are called to and the challenge many of us need strength to manage.

However sophisticated the computer software, there will still be a place for providence at the interface between prayer and visiting. If visiting becomes a routine bureaucratic procedure, like checking the gas meter, then the spirit will soon go out of it, and it will become meaningless. Providence is an honourable word. A more direct word might be 'hunch'. The dictionary definition of 'hunch' is 'something which pushes from within'. It is a prompt which says 'get up and go'. Having a wife or a husband who encourages you to act on these hunches can be very helpful. 'Go now, I'll put the supper in the oven' is so practical, but the simple Martha act is, ironically, worth hours of prayer.

Following this hunch can so frequently lead to being in the right place at the right time. I shall never forget one such visit. It was a Saturday afternoon, not the usual time for visiting, but I was pushed from within to go and see someone who, I must have known, was ill, but I did not know how seriously. I arrived. His wife let me in. He was certainly very ill, but I did not think that he was near death. We said the Lord's Prayer together. He said it very strongly in the cockney accent with which he used to announce the hymns from the back of the church every Sunday when he was well. The Lord's prayer was the last thing he said, and I was the last visitor he had. I am sure that this story could be told many times over by countless pastors through the centuries. God lets us know of the opportunities we can take.

There will be millions of opportunities we are unable to take. We shall just have to trust to the thought that God is far better at all this than we are. Where we have felt things have worked then it is not our skill but the movement of the Spirit which has been working with great delicacy and initiative. This gives the apostolic command 'go' a particular immediacy, an actual physical impetus, which is inspiringly captured in these words of Edward King, in an ordination address of 1869:

> Go wherever God may send you. Go without wishing to have everything arranged for your own tastes and your own comfort; without wishing to have everything in accordance even with your own religious desires. Go in the spirit of perfect self-surrender, of thorough self-devotion, simply for Christ. There should be no limit. Christ gives you your commission, and to Christ you must give it back.

Another story, this time from the earliest days of my school's community service group, which gave me my earliest experiences of going out to visit. The woman I was asked to visit seemed to me the oldest person possible in the world. She was bedridden and was dependent on meals on wheels. After visiting her for a while in her old ramshackle cottage, I realized the thing she needed was a bed table to go over her knees, to have her meals in bed. The woodwork department at school were happy to make this for her. The making of the table took an age, and I rather left going to visit her until it was ready. At last, two months later, it was finished, and I took it proudly round to her cottage. There was no reply at the door. The neighbour told me she had gone into hospital some time ago. I went straight to the geriatric ward of the local hospital clutching this bed table. I found the ward. The nurse on duty said that she had just died. It was a hard lesson to learn about the urgency of some visits. Prayer would have sharpened that urgency, perhaps given me a more insistent call when it was needed. I cannot say that I learnt the lesson completely, far from it, but it taught me about timing. 'Now is the hour.' Prayer can strengthen the will, and when it comes to a tussle between compassion and laziness, it is all too easy to be deaf to a call from the Holy Spirit.

On the other hand, we must not be paralysed by guilt, because it is humanly impossible to be in all places at once, and there are bound to be times when we simply cannot be at a particular place for a variety of reasons. If prayer is good for sharpening the will, it is also good for being where the body cannot be. There are examples in the Gospels where Jesus is not physically present with the sick, but he effects a cure. His reluctance to go immediately to Lazarus was surely for some good reason.

In the same way, though infinitely less powerful, prayer can travel. The basis of the contemplative religious life is that prayer leaps over the wall, and has an effect far beyond the confines of the bodies of those praying. There is much dispute over the effectiveness of the prayers of the saints on the well-being of those living, but the communion of saints, as traditionally represented, sets out in a general way the idea of a benign, spiritual influence which has its effect for good. With the huge growth of population, and increasing impossibility of visiting everyone in the parish, some theology of prayer which allows our love to reach where we cannot be, through Christ, would save us from a crippling sense of guilt we have about failure in this area. Stories from the past only add to this guilt.

The high watermark of parochial visiting was probably in the early part of this century, when communities knew their vicar and welcomed him in. This was before the massive rises in population and the fragmentation of communities, before the general sense of caution about other people and the general loss of faith in God. In 1947 Charles Forder was writing about parochial visiting: 'Solid visiting usually achieves ten to fifteen houses in the afternoon, and two hundred a month is suggested as a minimum. A quick revision campaign should include up to thirty in an afternoon, and about four hundred in a month.' If we take this to heart in our own day, then our prayers must be prayers of abject penitence for not managing anything like that. How they did it I do not know, but for the visit of one or one hundred we go in the spirit of God, fortified by the prayer we have struggled with in the times of preparation.

There often seems to be a tussle in the parochial ministry between action and contemplation, doing and being, being someone who prays or someone who visits, someone who gets out and about and someone who stays in. I was much cheered in thinking through this split by some words of Richard Meux Benson, parish priest and religious. Benson founded the Society of St John the Evangelist, in Cowley, in 1866. It was the first men's religious community in the Church of England since the Reformation, and it grew out of a parish ministry. It was a Mission Society. Benson was the vicar of Cowley, then a small settlement just outside Oxford. As he thought about this relationship of prayer and pastoral work, he was struck by its partnership rather than by its dichotomy:

> I cannot think that parochial work is in any way injurious to the strictest religious life. The real tasks of a parish – teaching in the school, visiting the poor and sick – are rather helpful to the spiritual life and are done all the better under the restrictions of timetable. The better organized a parochial system is, the more it will fit in with the monastic rule. Ministry to the children, the sick and poor has a spiritualising effect, leading the soul to God. Indeed a hard working curate has the advantage over us. For in all true parochial work there is a gradual learning of the power of the divine truth and its application to the needs of the individual soul. Nearness to God is not obtained by the mere absence of interruptions.

It is encouraging to think that it was the parish life that inspired and was the setting for this deepening of the religious life. That marriage of what seemed two opposites, prayer and visiting, could help us to revitalize our parishes in our own generation. Prayer will give depth to the pastoral work; and the daily contact with the needs of people will give life and meaning to prayer.

ii The visit

So we arrive on the doorstep, or at the side of the bed in the hospital ward. Not totally unprepared, of course, because there will be a minimal amount of background material we have to hand. We know the person, or we do not know them very well. They are members of the church. They are old, young, male or female, they have children, they haven't, they are children.

We also know why we are there. There are various usual reasons: exploratory, they are new residents in the parish. They are ill. They have a psychological problem. They are angry with the church over not being visited for a long time. They have some grudge. Their faith has been holed by redundancy or bereavement or marital problems. It is a social visit and you have been invited just to chat; or it is social plus, where the social aspect covers deeper areas which they want to share. They want something practical, like advice on funerals or headstones, or a book to read, or they just want to hand over a cake for the church sale. You have at least a minimal knowledge of who they are, and you have a reason for going. You are there, vulnerable, exposed, ready for almost anything.

Those visits where some special service is wanted, like home communion, anointing, laying on of hands, confessions, the ministry of deliverance, blessing of the house, take their course according to set forms that will be fairly standard and are not the subject of this chapter, although around each of these particular occasions there will be a chance to talk and share and develop a relationship.

One particularly helpful and vividly described picture of the home communion is found in an essay by Bishop Richard Holloway called 'By Way of Blackpool Tower', from a book *Stewards of the Mysteries of God* edited by Eric James (DLT 1979).

> I would come into her kitchen and take the little silver pyx out of the bag that hung round my neck and lay it between the lighted candles below the picture. For years I laid the sacrament of the body and blood of Christ beneath that photograph of Blackpool Tower.

A fascinating connection with the human life of Jesus is

woven round this photograph of Blackpool Tower, and all that he has to say about the incarnational aspect of visiting is very helpful.

The time together usually begins with 'small talk', the warm up, finding a seat, the weather, the news. I was told once that you should not make straight for the favourite seat of the deceased, and I think that is sound advice, although it is sometimes difficult to tell which that seat might have been. It shows insensitivity if you make yourself too much at home in a sensitive spot. As soon as the pleasantries have died down, a question which opens up the talk for the other person is useful. Even the straightforward 'How are you?' or 'How are things going?' tells them that they are the centre of your concern, and that you have time for them, and for them alone. That is why you are there, and you really do want to listen to what they have to say. To hear even a little of someone's background is to open up a window into their personality, which makes them so much more lovable. The slightest link is a helpful link.

It seems a commonplace now to say that we are there to listen to the person's story, but that is what it is. If we do not find other people's histories interesting, then pastoral work will be very heavy going indeed. We really do have to have an interest in others, and in letting their thoughts impinge on ours. An endless fascination with the variety of God's world is an essential qualification for successful visiting. Whenever possible and with not too heavy a hand, we can add bits of our story to theirs, but we should not try and cap every story of theirs with an even more interesting one of our own. Just enough of us to make them feel that they can listen and receive too, that they are not patients but companions. The psychiatrist's persistent 'hm . . . go on' does not seem quite to fill the bill for a parish visit. More conversational give-and-take seems to be required. We are listening and looking, keeping our antennae out so that we know that person well by the time it comes to leave. Hints can lead into a far deeper world. Photographs of Blackpool Tower tell a story by a glance, and the garden, if there is one, is always worth a walk round.

We watch during this time for signs of tiredness or anxiety, and we read them. Is it a restlessness of pain, or of guilt, or embarrassment? Have they had enough of us for this time? Is there something that they would really like to get off their chests now, or should it wait for another visit? Is it the baby's feeding time, or the favourite television programme? We listen for the way things are put. People often say profoundly religious things in non-religious language, and there is no need always to gear things round to the language that we feel comfortable with. Sometimes, because the vicar is there, a false religiosity appears which needs to be thawed out. At other times, to use the language that we are familiar with, which inevitably includes God, prayer, the Spirit, might just be what the other person needs to help them think through their own religious feelings. It might spark something deeply dormant in them, and kindle a flame of desire for God.

I tend to try and go at the other's pace. I would rather leave letting the person feel that they were listened to than put my spiritual agenda onto them too hastily. I think I err on the side of too little spiritual input; others may have the confidence for more. The spirituality could come as much in the sharing as in the teaching and praying, but as the time together draws to a close I gauge whether the time and the occasion seems right for a prayer. This is something of a crunch question, and by all accounts seems to be what this book is about, 'moments of prayer'. I hope I have managed to convey that more goes into this moment than just the minute or half a minute of the words themselves. The mechanics of this stage I shall be looking at in the next chapter, when the nature of words and their use in the pastoral situation is discussed.

The privilege of entering another person's life and home is always a sacred surprise. It involves a trust which prayer can hardly articulate but can hope to open out to God, either at the time of the visit or later. It allows a minister to have access to the depths of people's feelings and permission to be with them at the heights and depths of their family and personal experiences. We take the other into our hearts and love them. The poetry of pastoral experience is more often written on the minister's shoe leather than on his or her religious soul. We do it very badly, and day after day we wish to be more open to the miraculous possibilities that occur when we share the thoughts and hopes and fears of others. There is never an end to it, never an occasion when all the work is done. We can only take the bits and give thanks for that: 'giving thanks at all times and in all places'.

It is the people that make parish life. Although it can seem difficult and unrewarding when we are right in the middle of it, and there are so many things to think about we cannot relish any one thing in particular, looking back it will be the people we give thanks for. Not the paper, nor the bricks, nor the mowers, but the faces, the sheer physical thereness of the people. The great mystery and glory of the work is that we lead those people out of their physicality into the spiritual bodiliness of God's Kingdom. Our constant involvement with the passing over, or to put it plainly, death ('You must have seen a lot of that', they say), helps us to be there when the physical passes into the spiritual, and the great concourse of the communion of saints becomes a reality. Visiting, with its great nearness and solidity, is always moving towards a spiritual reality. The crossing over from one to another reality is a great mystery. It sparks our faith. It tests it. It draws out our emotions.

One of the great pastoral poems charts this emotion at the death of a Liverpool farrier, Felix Randal, from huge bodiliness to his anointed, resurrection being. Gerard Manley Hopkins, working in a parish in Liverpool at the time, brought lives and words into focus. Felix and Randal, sacraments of the person, his name, gave Hopkins the inspiration for the sound and feel of his poem:

This seeing the sick endears them to us, us too it endears.
My tongue had taught thee comfort, touch had quenched
    thy tears,
The tears that touched my heart, child, Felix, poor Felix
    Randal.

Prayer and words

When the time comes the Holy Spirit will
instruct you what to say.

Luke 12.12

—

We have to have the Minister
so the words will know where to go.

Anne Stevenson, 'Minister'

3

Prayer and words

i Plain words

It comes as no surprise to me that one of our greatest poets, George Herbert, should also be the most formative writer on the priest's life and work in *A Priest to the Temple, or The Countrey Parson his Character and Rule of Holy Life* (1652). The clerical profession has always been dealing in words. It has been its most obvious means of communicating the gospel, which was itself committed to words, by the Word, Jesus Christ.

We know now, and George Herbert's parishioners probably knew then, that touch and styles of life also communicate the gospel. What we say, formally in sermons and worship, informally in conversation, and in our writing, is a very important part of our work and witness. Words and language are important because they always represent more than themselves. In our words we open a window onto our souls.

In the Old Testament the Hebrew language, which is a robust one, delighting in the physical and material ways of putting deep truths, talks a lot about mouths and lips when it wants to stress the importance of language. 'Lord, open thou our lips, and our mouths shall show forth thy praise.' The guarding of the lips and the placing of words in the mouth by God are wonderfully vivid ways of putting language in its prime position. George Herbert loved words, and enjoyed using them to acknowledge his love of God, or of his Lord as he liked to say, and of his own inadequacy before God. His poems were written out of his own soul but he hoped they would be helpful to others.

Inevitably at times words fail us, but the minister is often called on to put into words what no one else can. The poet accomplishes this in verse, the minister does it very often in the faltering words of human experience. The minister also feels under an obligation to help others express their deepest feelings in their own words, to facilitate the movement of the tongue to praise; to pass the sound waves of the heart over the vibrating copper foil, and to worship. The minister's task is to tell the truth.

To use language to its best effect we have to be at home in it, but first we have to be in awe of it. We need to realize what a remarkable aspect of the human make-up it is, and how much words reflect the distinctive nature of being human. When God made the world, as described in Genesis 1, 'He spoke and it was done'. That creative word was an essential aspect of the nature of God, as understood by the writer of Genesis. Made in God's image, we too share that creative power of making or unmaking with our words. Prayer is the creative power of making an intimate relationship with God, and the language of prayer has itself been created through the centuries, into which tradition we step.

So, first, words are remarkable things. We use them so frequently, and look at them so often, that they cease to amaze us. Just think about them for a moment. What are they? They are a mixture of letters, but not any letters put any way in any order. They are built up purposefully to indicate something. In this sense, they are sound pictures. They have a meaning. If I say the word 'Jesus', I am conveying a picture, an idea, a life, a person. I am also sparking off in the reader or listener, a whole lot of memories, thoughts, feelings, which might be quite different from what my pictures or thoughts are. At its simplest level, the single word will reverberate, and since Jesus was what he was the reverberations, the meaning, will convey goodness and truth, peace and light. There are a whole range of words, which by their meaning and their use generally convey the healing power of goodness, not arbitrarily, but through the deeply honest and loving reality which they embody. The names for God, I believe, stand in this category, particularly the names of the Trinity of persons: Father, Son and Holy Spirit. There was quite a strong theological tradition to meditate and write commentaries on the names of God.

The fervour with which religious people protect the holiness of the name of their God is a clear indication of the power that name holds for them. They are not just words, they are words with a history, a meaning and a power. A crisis in the power of the word in our own generation has made it very difficult for some to reconcile themselves to the paternalism inherent in the male God. For some it so radically skews the sense of the divine in the human, male metaphor that the words become unusable, and we go through the process of learning new words. Generally, though, a word takes on a patina, a lichen of goodness. So much so that in the Orthodox tradition of the Jesus prayer, the name of Jesus is enough for prayer. The name is said repeatedly until it is incorporated into the person's whole being. Single words can have this power.

We are rarely satisfied with the single word. With increasing subtlety and sophistication of thought and communication we branch out into a string of words, and, all of a sudden, new worlds are opened up, new possibilities are discovered, new problems are raised. We set beside the pure adoration of the name 'Jesus', the claim that 'Jesus is Lord'. In doing this we colonize a whole world of thought about power, ruling, supremacy, commitment and obedience. The phrase 'Jesus is Lord' is shorthand for a statement of personal belief. We are into deep waters, and for many happily so. As we swim out from the single word Abba, or Jesus, or God, or Spirit, and wish to wrap more meaning around these words, what are we doing? Have we the confidence to share these words, and how do we respond to the words of others who are trying to communicate thoughts, beliefs, feelings to us?

Two sidelights here come to mind. The first is the memory of how difficult it was to say out loud, and in public, the word

God in days when others might laugh at it or accuse you of being 'religious' or ostracize you for it. In some countries and some places this still happens, but even in our own lives there was probably a time when this gulf had to be crossed. The power of the word and the significance for us of its use needs to be brought back to us occasionally when after years of its use in public worship we have rubbed the coin of holy words smooth. It takes the writer or the poet to remind us of the special quality of language, those for whom each word will resonate and be drawn from the store of fresh language. Our poets working on the edge of language, and conscious of the space surrounding words, are able to restore to us the original power of a word.

I labour through these things because we often rush into language just to fill an awkward silence, and fail to wonder at the great gift of words, their power to heal and their power to destroy, to move us to tears, and to make us laugh, to express the depths of disgust and the heights of exaltation, and, as we share in the poets' words, to see language dancing, or trekking on the edges of experience, pushing the boundaries of language out into uncharted territory. Surely, we say, hasn't every human experience been written about by now? What is new? It is remarkable how a good writer is able to create something unique, by putting the reality of their own vision into the mix of words and rhythms and by omitting as much as adding. It is as if such writers find their own 'voice', not as they slavishly copy the style or voice of another, that the magic or alchemy or transfiguration of language occurs.

To what extent does this discussion of language ring true for the words we use in what seems like the quite casual conversations that we have with others? The psalmist reminds us of the sanctity of words and the caution which follows from that sanctity. He held his tongue in a world which was not honouring God. He refrained from speaking out. In the end his sense of the urgency of proclaiming the truth, and his earnestness for righteousness, caused him to speak, but there was a real struggle of conscience. In a world of so many unnecessary words, the witness of silence, the restraint and the discipline of silence, provides an eloquent redress. The restraint of the tongue is a constant theme of the Wisdom literature, and seems to have far more a priority in the Old Testament than the restraint of any other part of the body.

Words are also sacraments. They are the outward and visible sign of an inward and spiritual grace, and the reverence with which we deal with official or recognized sacraments should spill over into our dealings with these other more common ones, like language. The Jews are so aware of the majesty of God that they do not use the name, as such. 'Jahweh' is the English transliteration of the Hebrew letters which are substituted for the Divine Name. Coming from a rather different direction, the Danish theologian, Søren Kierkegaard, recommended like the Gadarenes of the gospel that we beg Christ to depart from us (Luke 8.37). This sounds rather extreme, but it is in reaction to an over-familiarity with the severe nature of what Christ is, and the values he represents. We need to be brought up sharply to realize how demanding Christianity actually is. Words can be so softened that we forget the sharpness of the meaning they represent.

Having said that, when it comes to oiling the wheels of ordinary social gatherings and making contact with people, words are a great help. The person with no small talk finds getting in touch with others very difficult. Other people are put off, they sense that they are going to have to do all the work. The rules of the social game are not so far removed from the rules of ordinary compassion when you try to speak to someone to put them at their ease. In public situations like railway trains the English have traditionally found this extremely difficult.

The question of what you say when you go to visit someone, the sheer and simple mechanics of conversation, is something that after years of practice we take for granted, and perhaps need to have some self-critical thought about. Perhaps we have become too slick. At the beginning it is a necessary skill to learn. The basic principle must be the welfare of the other, and the best advice is to be yourself, to offer yourself as openly and sensitively as possible to others.

It is important to put the other at their ease and to help them feel secure, wanted and that they matter, so that they are in a position to feel at ease with themselves. Words can help this process, as can the tone of voice and the space we create for listening to the other. The right word often comes from the listening heart.

Paradoxically, the value of staying for a while in a silent religious community to learn the power of words is immense. The formal silence takes away the compulsion to talk, relaxes you and allows you to feel the presence of God's loving affirmation, regardless of what you say or how you show up in public. The huge burden of compulsory small talk is lifted. The professional hazard of the clergy is often having to be on the edge of conversations which are lacking in any sense of reality, or are subsidiary to what might in any sense be considered the real thing. The silent time of refreshment can be a great blessing here.

What we are driving at is, I suppose, appropriate language and appropriate silence, words as an aid to the pastoral relationship, and silence assisting the mechanics of communication and providing the refreshment in between the words. Put in that context, prayer comes as the heightening of that language and the placing into our being with others words which suit.

What words suit? Essentially we feel for them, and gauge the situation. Someone who is dying may appear not to hear, but might be well able to; someone very much alive might just need the sense of a silent presence. Those in very great distress sometimes need the comfort of a down-to-earth chat, and some will need the well-placed simple word of wisdom. As we understand the depth of God's love for us in the silence, so we are equipped to be sensitive to the balance of words and silence in our time with others.

The framing of most conversations happens automatically. By the time we are adult we have learnt the mechanics of it, but I can still remember the painful process of learning to time jokes, or knowing what to say at a time it would not be shot down in flames or laughed at. There was always the fear of saying the wrong thing. It was often better to say nothing at all and to keep one's counsel. We underestimate the pain and struggle which many go through to say anything. Training in theological colleges in the 1960s was much concerned with working in groups, to become more sensitive to the ebb and flow of language and silence as an indication of a person's feelings. We were taught to listen creatively and to respond sensitively. One great criticism of the professional pastor is if he or she does not seem to know how to listen. We ask God often enough to listen to us, we should in return learn how to listen both to God and to others, and to the God in others. Experience inevitably helps, as we grow in compassion for others and are prepared to keep learning, to curb impatience and to enlarge our hearts.

Occasionally, and hopefully rarely, it will not be a conversation we are involved in, but abuse. We will be shouted at and in receipt of the blind rage of someone who is deeply hurt. We are the nearest to hand, the first rock for the wave to break on. Automatic reactions come into play, which hopefully will be just absorbing the random anger, although it can be deeply troubling at the time. Curiously, those who use us to vent their anger can be the ones who are most committed to us in the long run.

Words in pastoral situations are a sort of prayer. They are attempting to communicate something of the love of God, however thinly. At the normal tempo of conversation there is no need to be consciously 'religious', although sometimes the word you wish you had not said is the one that is remembered. Hopefully the intention of good will beneath the language is picked up. Then there will come a time when you wonder if it would be right to say a prayer, either a formal prayer well known to the one being visited or one made up for the occasion. Some visitors would not feel it right to leave without a prayer, and there is a very strong case for ending all visits with prayer, but not all feel comfortable with such a rigid rule. Some gauge the occasion, the need and the level of spiritual awareness of the one they are visiting. What is actually going on here, in this very private area of visiting, we shall deal with next.

51

ii Turning words into prayers

We are trying to help people travel more deeply into God. We have the tremendous privilege of sharing in that journey, of being channels of God's peace, and of co-operating with the Holy Spirit who is the inspiration and prayer within us. Paul's words here about prayer are helpful. Paul recognized that the Spirit prays within us, sometimes with groans and gasps and sighs, because we simply do not know what to say (Romans 8.26). Words fail us. That is putting it at its most difficult. I am sure Paul would say it was not always like that, but it is a good reminder that we should expect some struggle in what is a most demanding process.

Words, however, do not always fail us, and very often it seems right and appropriate to pray with and for another. I sense that is true, but it is difficult to know for sure. There are no easy, all-purpose rules about it. I sometimes do and sometimes do not. I sense whether the other person will feel comfortable to accept a spoken prayer, whether they are likely to be used to it and will not be frightened or confused by it. The quality of the talk that is being engaged in is also an indication. If it has been of a deep and personal nature, on matters that have involved quite a a bit of pain and heart-searching, and difficult territory has been opened up, then the ground is well dug and watered for prayer. If there is illness or tiredness, or vulnerability, or mental disturbance, then a quiet and calming time with a few words of divine comfort can be very helpful and healing. Sometimes the quality of the time has been so profound that words seem unnecessary, and a prolonged period of silence with a final grace and a thanks to each other and to God might seem appropriate.

The place, too, will have its effect. Some places help us into praying together, places where it seems the natural and right thing to do, places with the necessary seclusion and privacy and the all-important right atmosphere. There will be other times when the talk needs to be lightened, or defused, when it has become too 'religious', and a prayer as a conclusion might simply reinforce a problem. This might seem casual to

some readers, but it is not meant to be. Rather it is an attempt
to respond to the individuality of each person and occasion as
seems appropriate. Prayer can be an act of extreme intimacy,
and if we feel unable to conclude that time with an act of
prayer, then that needs to be understood and not a cause for
guilt on either side. There will be some people who we find
it difficult to pray with, for the very best of reasons. It could
be assuming too much, catching someone on the wrong foot,
too soon in the relationship, too dominant.

Here again it may seem too diffident, too unprofessional,
too much laid open to the subjective whim of the pastor.
Some will see the minister or pastor, in role, as quite clearly
the person with whom you pray, and no doubt about it.
Would the Curé d'Ars, a French priest who saw huge
numbers of penitents every day, decide in each situation and
with each person whether or not he would say a prayer with
them? The value of set forms of confession, or prayer in pastoral situations, is that it can be free of the personal decision,
but I would imagine that the Curé d'Ars would be listening
out for the subtleties of response needed for each person
and administering the words in proportion to the ability of
the other to receive them. The Abbé Monnin, the Curé
d'Ars' mentor, said that 'in spiritual direction the chief thing
is to follow God's call and make others follow it, to keep pace
with the Holy Spirit, to proportion oneself to souls in order
to make them conform to Jesus Christ'.

This process of 'proportioning oneself to souls' is what I
have been trying to say about the sensitivity needed in asking
people to cope with the words that make up our prayer. As
the clarity of the role of pastors or ministers has been blurred
in the late twentieth century, their position has become much
more complex. It is not always so straight down the line.
Having said that, in a great many of the pastoral situations we
deal with as ministers of the gospel, a time of prayer at its
conclusion will be expected.

If it seems right to suggest a moment of prayer, after a short
pause to still the mind and the body and to centre the mind
in the heart, I begin with words that come from a store deep

within, guarded and stocked by the Holy Spirit, and usually they are terribly simple. I try and sum up in one or two brief phrases the issues that have been on our minds and in our hearts, and offer them to God. I pray for the person I am with and bless them: 'O Lord, bless this your servant, hold her in your arms, comfort her, heal her, give her strength, bless her family.' I will pray it and mean it, and love the person through my words, and sense the closeness of the Lord Jesus who is there despite all the fumbling of vocabulary and the awkward position by the hospital bed.

A prayer of healing I often use with the laying on of hands on the head, is this one:

> The healing mercies of the risen Lord, Jesus Christ,
> who is present here with us now,
> enter into your soul, your mind, your body,
> and heal you from all that harms you,
> and give you his peace.

The ability to remember prayers by heart is a great gift, and the additional ability to draw from the memory a prayer or psalm that absolutely suits the situation is also a great help. The need to speak the remembered prayer without 'gush' as if it had been written for that person in that situation is the art. The Holy Spirit helps us to find words from the heart, but like any creative process it needs to be self-critical, and the clichés cleaned up by the cleansing power of contemplative silence.

I conclude with a well-known prayer like the Lord's Prayer, or the Grace, which the other can join in if at all possible. If, at moments of grave illness, and the one being visited is able to say a few words, I work quite hard to help them share in the words of the Lord's Prayer, which means of course going extremely slowly, and could mean only one phrase, together. And then the silence, the space, to let God resound. Those pauses, before the world rushes back in, can be numinous, especially if you realize that you are not guiding the silence, but are being guided and served by the very one you were commissioned to save, and that the relationship has become mutual, in Christ.

How easy it is to forget the real world when we sit in our studies and pontificate about what we should or should not do in moments of pastoral care, with regard to specifically spiritual matters. The kids are screaming, the dogs barking, there is a knock at the door, the telephone rings, and you are trying to explain the finer points of baptism into the name of the Holy Trinity to a mum who rarely, if ever, goes to church. What place does prayer have in this situation? Probably none. It is just not the right and suitable time for prayer. Why not? What does it say about prayer if it is not suitable in this circumstance? Baptism visits are often with parents, or one parent, whose links with the church and with God are fairly slim. They know they want something that might be described as 'God' or 'church' or 'vicar', and in terms of feelings want something which we might describe as affirmation and a sense of the goodness and power of God over this child and in them, but the circumstances of the visit in the home might not make it easy or possible to have even a moment's quiet. That has to be engineered in some way at some different time: in the evening when there is help with the children, or the child is asleep. Some time in which a moment's reflection is possible, the television can be turned off, and God can offer himself with the still, small voice. At first, it is very short, but slowly the confidence grows and the opportunities for deeper prayer can be made.

What sort of a God then am I picturing? A God who can only work in the quiet, and not a God who can bring quiet, or shout above the hubbub or even be in the hubbub? God only in the lay-by and not on the motorway? When Jesus was curing the 12-year-old girl, Jairus's daughter, he asked for peace (Matthew 9.23–25). Elijah, when he was contesting with the worshippers of Baal, did not hear the Lord of thunder, but the God of the whisper (1 Kings 19.12). It is difficult to hear God if you cannot hear yourself, and a prayer, which is a distillation of the will of God, an acknowledgement of the presence of God, needs a space. The constant sense of bustle and noise in the domestic environment makes it very difficult for that sense of the sacred to get a foothold. As ministers we often have to come back at another time, to find it and help others experience it.

A couple want to get married. They make an appointment to see the vicar. They come. They know what they want, and the advice they want to hear is limited to the number of hymns and how much room for manoeuvre the photographer is allowed. The reception, the dress, the mother-in-law, the photographs loom large. I sense in this situation that the 'fear' of God or humility before God is missing. I see them. I see them again. I get to know them. There are cracks in the armour. Things are not that simple. There is a sense of not knowing, of vulnerability. I try through listening and talking and going through the words of the service to convey some sense of another dimension to life, other than the purely material one. I try and say that without looking outwards together to God the human love which seems so strong might falter. To limit the concern for this to a shared prayer at the end of the session might make them feel that religion is just something tacked on, the formal bit at the end which they might expect from being in a rectory for the marriage preparation. Weddings are some of the most difficult situations to let God in. They are very busy times. There is a lot of nervous emotion flying about. They are set up as such a this-world occasion. Yet we do have the honour and privilege of guiding two people preparing for the great day in church. We rehearse the service, and that usually allows for a few moments together, to have a final word and to let God in, to ask for his strength and guidance, asking him to work through our lives with his Holy Spirit.

Hospital visits, home visits, baptism visits, wedding interviews, all demand their own particular moments of prayer. The sensitivity of the minister has to catch the moment, use it to let God in and to transform occasions, and then lives. If it is impossible to pray at the time, back home there will be time and space.

iii The prayers of others

Although the word 'prayer' is now used to cover a great deal of ground which might previously have been called 'Christian life' or meditation, originally its use was fairly narrowly confined to words spoken to God, mainly in the form of asking. There is a danger that nowadays we over spiritualize prayer and imagine that the best prayer is silent adoration. There is certainly a very important place for word-less prayer, as I have been saying perhaps with too great a frequency here, but what about those prayers which are very much words, glorious, helpful, inspiring words in which others have encapsulated a particular thought about the Christian life, and are actually asking for things?

In the Anglican tradition the prayers, and particularly the collects, are perhaps the best known and best loved of such prayers. The prayers of the Book of Common Prayer gener-ally came through a much older source, and were a translation from Latin into the English of the day, at a time when the English language was vigorous, sinewy and graceful. Former generations learnt these prayers by heart. They were a common store of ways of talking to God. People felt comfortable with their familiarity. They had shape, and a particular beginning and end, secure against the vagaries of individual interpreta-tion, forgetting perhaps that each prayer had hidden within it its own particular theology. Such rock-like security in the written prayer led Eric Milner White, Provost of King's College, Cambridge, and later Dean of York, to write: 'Thus the Church gained a tongue meet for celestial service; and away from the language of the Bible, Prayer Book, or some approximation to their standard, the Englishman is never comfortable for long in public prayer.' The effect and influ-ence of the public prayers of the Church have filtered down for many into the private sphere, and here too people feel more comfortable with a prayer they know than with one that could go on longer and take more emotional turns than they can manage.

This, I realize, is a matter of temperament and tradition. In

David Hare's play *Racing Demon*, in which he presents a particular team of clergy in the Church of England, there is a
scene in which the Team Rector prays with a young woman
who is in distress. After a rather short and embarrassed few
words of prayer, the young woman says in a surprised and sad
voice, 'Is that it?' The eager curate, looking on as part of his
instruction, declares rather tartly, 'It was very low-key'. Some
expect considerably more in their time of prayer with another
than a beautiful but brief collect.

It is not only the Book of Common Prayer that provides
us with a store of memorable prayers. We slip quite easily into
the prayers of others and make them our own: 'O Lord, make
me an instrument of thy peace . . .', 'Teach me, good Lord, to
give and not to count the cost . . .', so much so that the
authorship of such prayers seems to be irrelevant. They are
just part of the tradition, the store of stuff that we know, and
because we know them so well we can share them with
others most easily.

They are frequently collected into anthologies of prayers.
Collections of prayers have been made from the early days of
Christian history. Many people make up their own anthology
as a resource for their own prayers, and for pastoral situations.
You could say 'of the collecting of prayers there seems to be
no end'. Many of these anthologies are available in small
pocket-sized editions so they can be used on journeys, or in
hospital, or in battle. To see the much thumbed and annotated
copies of people's personal prayer collections is very moving.
They are built up over years. Prayers are cut out and pasted
in, written out in scrawl or copper-plate, interspersed with
notes or even shopping lists. There is a neat serendipity when
such collections get lost and then are found years later, or, in
the case of Thomas Traherne's *Centuries*, three hundred years
later, on a second-hand book barrow.

One of the most famous and highly regarded commonplace
books of prayers is that by Lancelot Andrewes (1555–1626),
and is usually referred to as his *Private Prayers*. The particular
genius of Andrewes' collection is that it stays as close as it
can to scriptural material, while at the same time making

something new of it. Part of the collection is ordered under the time-honoured headings of adoration, penitence, intercession and thanksgiving, and there is material of this sort for each day of the week. Each day has an introductory meditation based on the story of creation in Genesis 1.

To see the way Andrewes handles the great body of scriptural material, so deftly and with such integrity and personal involvement, is a great example. To pray through the Scriptures is to bring alive prayer, Scripture and ourselves. It was Andrewes' unique position, rather like Shakespeare, to live at the crossroads of the medieval and modern worlds, and in that crucible where the catholic and the reformed traditions were remoulding themselves.

Prayers, unlike much other literature, seem to be common property. They get changed a little bit here and there, people forget whose they are, or who wrote them. In fact their anonymity is sometimes a help because then we can concentrate on their meaning rather than their authorship.

Scripture means many things to many people, but this discussion reminds us that it is also a prayer book. It contains the prayers of many biblical characters, many of them from the Old Testament, as well as the prayers of Jesus and Paul from the New Testament. It is in the prayers of these great figures that we often find a summary of their thought – in the same way that if we were asked to have one prayer, we would try and encapsulate our main concern as well as our general attitude to God. Prayers are very telling things. When it came to Jesus being asked to teach his disciples to pray, he too gave a summary of his main concerns and his thoughts about God. So there came about what we call the Lord's Prayer. It is not the only prayer Jesus prayed, but it is an excellent summary of things that would have been much on his mind and heart in regard to God, his Father.

Christ's prayer is essentially a dialogue with the Father, an intimate discourse with his Father, 'Abba'. Though neatly summarized in the Lord's Prayer, we assume that in the day-to-day reality of Jesus' life, that prayer was drawn out into its separate strands and lived and prayed through at length.

'Our Father in heaven' sets the scene in adoration, in love and in acknowledgement of the holiness of God the Father. 'Your Kingdom come' expresses the longing for the reign of God to exist in time, and highlights Jesus' own mission to proclaim the Kingdom of God as present, in the acts of healing and the process of teaching. 'Your will be done' continues the Kingdom theme in all its complexity of here and hereafter. The bread of the day is asked for, real bread which feeds the hungry, and the bread of heaven which feeds the spiritually hungry. Tussling with forgiveness and sin, Jesus shows the reciprocity of forgiveness, 'Forgive us as we forgive'. Finally, Christ asks for the great test of the final catastrophe, brought on by human sin, to be spared for the faithful.

The Lord's Prayer is a summary of the prayer of Christ, as the Mosaic Ten Commandments are summarized by Christ into the twofold command of love of God and love of our neighbour. The Lord's Prayer reaches out into a life of prayer and service which has for its impetus the desire to do the will of God. This desire in Jesus was fostered in the hills by night and a long time before dawn, on the lake, in the wilderness and in the home of Mary, Martha and Lazarus at Bethany. The Lord's Prayer is the great model prayer, and as we pray it we can imagine Jesus saying the same words.

It takes some time to get into the meaning and heart of a prayer, and to make it one's own. Perhaps when you first hear it, there is a phrase which grips your attention, and you wonder where it comes from so that you can look at it again. People quite frequently ask me, 'You know that prayer about the shadows lengthening and the evening comes. Where would I find it?' It is obviously a night prayer, but is also suitable for a time of bereavement, and in preparation for death. Those two areas of light, the night and death, often coincide in prayer. This particular prayer is found in the Alternative Service Book under 'A selection of additional prayers which may be used at Funerals' and is also attributed to John Henry Newman:

> O Lord, support us all the day long of this troublous life, until the shades lengthen, and the evening comes, and the

busy world is hushed, the fever of life is over, and our work is done. Then, Lord, in your mercy grant us safe lodging, a holy rest, and peace at the last; through Jesus Christ our Lord.

The point is, I think, that many people are helped by remembering a particular prayer. Words matter to them when the meaning strikes home, when it speaks to their condition; and all the better if that prayer has a telling use of language, or a balance in its structure, or a rhythm which assists the meaning. The difference between poetry and prayer, or should we say the relation between poetry and prayer, is a big subject, but suffice it to say a prayer can have some of the elements of a good poem, and some poems are written as prayers, and some poems make good prayers. It is a flexible relationship. Gerard Manley Hopkins' poem 'Glory be to God for dappled things' makes an excellent grace before meals. The language of prayer is obviously important, but it is most frequently the intention of a prayer which makes it a helpful or an unhelpful one. When the two harmonize, meaning and language, and the rhythm is part of it too, then we get the classic prayers, remembered and loved by many:

> God be in my head
> and in my understanding,
> God be in my eyes
> and in my looking,
> God be in my mouth
> and in my speaking,
> God be in my heart
> and in my thinking,
> God be at my end
> and at my departing.
> (*The Sarum Primer*, 1558)

When they asked
'How shall we pray?' He answered:
'Does the seed ask: how shall I pray?
It enters into its closet, shuts its door,
And prays in secret, as if not praying,
and fasts as if not fasting, till
it grows into a flower, and prays
not with words, but through fragrance.'
Gopal Singh, *The Man Who Never Died*

—

4

Prayer and the professionals

Recently, attending a course on 'learning outcomes' in adult education, I very forcefully came up against the need to be very clear as to what it was I was trying to do and what it was that I wanted from those I was teaching. This was partly so that my teaching would be more positive, planned and directed, and partly so that its effectiveness could be tested in terms of how successfully those being taught had fulfilled the aims and benefited from the negotiated aims of the course. Professionalism and assessment are the educationalists' words of the decade.

In the light of this there always seems to be hanging over the question of prayer and visiting the two spectres of 'professionalism' and 'assessment'. How does this random, seemingly spirit-directed activity of prayer tie in with the professional world of counselling? How can we tell what we are doing, and evaluate whether we are doing it well or badly? First of all, though, a bigger and even more intractable question: what actually are we trying to achieve?

In the world of the spirit, there are no easily defined edges. It compares, in that regard, to the world of the arts and philosophy and creativity in general. What is a poet doing when he or she writes a poem? What is one Christian doing for another Christian when he or she listens to them and prays with them? Both are trying to produce something of value. Both are responding to given material in a sensitive and creative way. Both wait on inspiration.

The way of describing the action of prayer in a pastoral situation also lays itself open to vagueness. 'Prayer', said Thomas

Merton, 'often looks like idleness.' It is very difficult to say what is going on, partly because of its spiritual nature and partly because the language in which we describe it has its own chemistry. If we describe it without some element of the poetic, we are likely to miss the essence of prayer as a multi-layered and luminous experience. It works, as Gopal Singh said, in the same way as a flower.

When Jesus was trying to describe the nature of the Kingdom of God, he came across a similar problem of language. To pin the nature of the Kingdom down, in the language of weights and measures, or in the strict definitions of the Law, would be to abuse the very mysterious nature of the Kingdom itself, which Jesus knew had to remain closed to idle scrutiny but remain accessible to faith. He had to describe the Kingdom by use of images, stories, parables and by anecdote. For example: 'If a woman has ten silver coins and loses one of them, does she not light the lamp, sweep out the house, and look in every corner till she finds it?' (Luke 15.8). This parable describes the process, and its earnestness of looking for the Kingdom. The finding of the coin is cause for great rejoicing, as is the discovery of the presence of God. With regard to prayer, the parable of the importunate widow (Luke 18.1–8) is Jesus' way of describing the need to keep praying and never to lose heart.

If asked to explain myself with regard to prayer in the pastoral situation I would begin with a word like 'gathering'. In the unspoken, emotional world that surrounds two people in conversation about the things of the spirit, there comes a time when prayer becomes the helpful gatherer-up of thoughts and feelings and insights. Prayer can take all that and lay it before God, the gathered-up gifts of a time together.

The Spirit will have been blowing where it will, in all the ups and downs of struggled attempts to say how we feel. Lots of bits of emotion will have been flying about in all sorts of ways, inside a person and outside, emotions which can be recognized but not easily tied down or quantified, described but not completely captured. We sense the presence of God, the presence of evil. We are on the edge of despair, but we do not know how near, or what is over the edge. Our bodies are weak, limp, close to tears, ready to speak out in anger, longing to be held, but not sure of the protocol or the dangers. However much we may know of these things, however much experience we have had of similar settings in the past, we come to each meeting freshly. The minister, the one who feels responsible for how the whole thing is going, becomes a channel, a gatherer, an orderer, a receiver of the power that the raw material of sound, word, feeling is giving out. We sense the need to make an order out of that, and direct it as best we can. We bring all that we are, all that we have been, all that we would like to be, to the edge of the eye of the needle, and we compose ourselves to thread all that through into the space beyond. We sometimes find it as difficult as Huckleberry Finn did when, dressed in disguise as a girl, he was trying to look confident threading a needle.

I have said that praying has in it the element of general creativity, but there is one difference, I feel, between the work of the artist and the work of the minister when we are think-ing of this creative, gathering process. The poet has words for his or her task. The minister has an even more intractable and elusive thing. It is often described in personal terms as the Holy Spirit. It is the power we call on which we feel to be greater than ourselves. The minister feels powerless without it. Yet although we sense we have only ourselves, 'ourselves' includes the capacity to call for help on the Holy Spirit.

The self is crucial, but only the self in its humility to acknowledge the need of God. Naturally diffident over our talents in this area, there is a wisdom which says 'be someone worth knowing'. Dangerous as that may sound if taken wrongly, rightly understood it gives us a responsibility to be people who are always preparing to be the instruments of God's love, of his healing and his teaching. The great spiritual writer Evelyn Underhill (1875–1941) was much concerned to say that it was the quality of the life of prayer in a priest that made all the difference: 'To do great things for souls, you must become the agent and channel of a more than human love, and this must be the chief object of a

65

priest's life of prayer' (*The Parish Priest and the Life of Prayer*, Mowbray, 1938).

We learn to be such channels in solitude; we practise it in community. We learn it in the silence of our rooms where God is in secret (Matthew 6.6). We go out with fear and trembling to meet the other, to be someone for that person, for good, for building them up in love and health. It is felt as a power, a strengthening. It is a pentecostal fact, 'They were all filled with the Holy Spirit' (Acts 2.4), and an annunciatory fact, 'the power of the Most High will overshadow you' (Luke 1.35).

Reginald Somerset Ward (1881–1962) writes helpfully about spiritual direction, and this elusive quality of 'power':

A priest cannot make bricks without straw, he cannot do his work without power. If he is to have power it must come through the soul to the mind and will . . . the source of all the power which is ever to be found in the life of a priest is God the Holy Ghost. (*His Life and Letters*, Mowbray 1963)

Writing in an era when power was massively abused, the word has become an uneasy one. We are happier with Paul's gloss on it when he says that our power is made perfect in weakness (2 Corinthians 12.9). Certainly, as we acknowledge our own failures, vulnerability and frailty, 'the ministry of the empty hands', and as we reflect on them, and try to do something about them, then our ministering will have that edge of power perfected in weakness. These are the necessary chinks in the armour which allow others the delight of knowing that we are as human as they are. This wonderful power, or grace, is built up by our own wanting it, needing it, and longing for it from God. So, not by our own efforts, but by our own hand in hand with God's we become ministers 'worth knowing'.

In *The Diary of a Country Priest* by George Bernanos, the priest has a difficult time in the parish, but slowly he wins the hearts of his people, until visiting one of his most recalcitrant parishioners who is approaching death he has this conversation:

I [the priest] was watching for a smile of scorn, or at least
of pity on those wilful lips – I feared his pity more than his
scorn.
— You're a good lad, he said at last, I wouldn't want any
priest but you around when I was dying.
And he kissed me, as children do, on both cheeks.

What we are actually doing in prayer, on our own or with
others, will never be known for sure. We are trying to be
available, to make space, to empty our hands so that Christ
may fill them with his work. We have to live with that sometimes frustrating sense of not knowing the outcome, of not
reaping the harvest. We shall reap the harvest of other people's
sowing, others will gather in our grain. Prayer itself, so full of
the air of the Spirit, will remain elusive, and its fruits too will
not easily be counted on a points basis. Faith is our best ally
here.

Having said how difficult a thing prayer is to describe, and
that the minister has the intricate task of gathering it out of
the air and threading it into eternity, can we say how this
process differs from the skills of the professional counsellor?
Are we only doing, in an amateur way, what others are
trained and certified to do for money, for a living? There has
been a great growth in the counselling world over the last
thirty years. At theological college in the 1960s we were
beginning to absorb its insights and its influence in our group
work, and our contacts with psychiatric departments of hos-
pitals and in our reading list of psychology books. People have
found it enormously helpful to have a counselling service
which is seemingly free of any religious or moral overtones,
in which listening and understanding does not come with a
ticket labelled 'God'. This is because, for many, God has been
the problem. Psychotherapy cannot solve all our problems
but it has helped people look at themselves and see how they
relate to that self and to others. Analysts are used to such
experiences and can listen without raised eyebrows or
embarrassment. Great expertise has been built up. It has
become a subject in its own right, a world of its own with a

language of its own. It makes the half hour of free wisdom from the minister look in some ways unprofessional, and for some there is a sense of 'If I don't pay for it, can it be any good?'

Enormous benefits can be got from the professional world of counselling, built as it is on a more 'scientific' understanding of the person. It provides a technical language to indicate the derivation and subtleties of mood and behaviour. It has given us pictures of ourselves which present our histories, our stories, our drives and our hopes in a new light to us. Very often these insights and the language will run parallel with the wisdom of the past, and with specifically religious insights. To be familiar with both old and new worlds can be a great help in the work of assisting people see the problems of their lives.

The minister, however, has a particular responsibility for what has traditionally been called the soul. The soul is a particularly unbiological and unclassifiable organ. Like God on the astronaut's journey, it does not seem to be there, but it is a felt reality by those who believe. The soul is what we are about, our area of expertise. Before looking at the dictionary I will give a definition of my own: the soul is that part of us which responds to God. A further refinement is that we feel we cannot have engineered this soul for ourselves, and so God puts it in us, so that we can use it to respond to him. Sensing the soul in another is made easier by knowing the soul in ourselves. Soul speaks to soul. We image it rather like a heart, since we often sense a strong relationship between the soul and the heart. The soul feels like a central thing. Different from the heart though, it picks up vibrations other than just our emotions. It has also a mind-quality to it, a sensible, thinking bit, but again it holds secrets independent of the mind. If God is ultimately different from us, although part of us, then that which receives him and responds to him will retain its unique identity but remain within us.

I am reminded of the black box flight recorders that aeroplanes carry to record the details of their flight. They can be used after crashes because they have preserved crucial details, they hold the secrets, the story. So we have a soul to record our story, the way we are in the eyes of God. So when we say 'How is your soul?' we are really wanting to know how is your relationship with God. The language is specialized, as specialized seemingly as the language of psychotherapy. Some will feel comfortable in one, others in another, and there will be helpful people who can speak both languages and translate. Yet is there something lying behind the language of the soul that indicates a different area of experience in which the minister can be particularly helpful, in a way the psychotherapist might not be, or might not be in the same way?

I am conscious, as I go along, that the language of the soul is not very precise. It works with images and stories, and not in the language of fact. It will sound 'unscientific'. It approximates more to the language of the Scriptures, and to the experience of that remarkable group of wise people known as the Desert Fathers and Mothers of the third and fourth centuries who lived, away from the cities, in the Egyptian desert. They continued and inspired a whole genre of wisdom writing which stretches much wider than just Egypt. These desert sages provide just a small collection of the holy wisdom which has been available in all generations from those who walk with God. We think of the scriptural book of the Proverbs, and Wisdom in the Apocrypha. They teach the secrets of the soul in stories, often humorous, because when the pride of human beings comes up against the glory of God, there is often hubris, the unexpected, almost the clownish. For such people the language of the soul seems like second nature:

A brother asked one of the elders: what good thing shall I do, and have life thereby? The old man replied: God alone knows what is good. However, I have heard it said that someone inquired of Father Abbot Nisteros the great, the friend of Abbot Anthony, asking: What good work shall I do? and that he replied: Not all works are alike. For Scripture says that Abraham was hospitable and God was with him. Elias loved solitary prayer, and God was with him. And David was humble, and God was with him.

Therefore, whatever you see your soul to desire according to God, do that thing, and you shall keep your heart safe. (Thomas Merton, *The Wisdom of the Desert* (New Directions 1970), p. 25)

The soul is the yearning part of us. 'Us' as we really are, because it is our maker's part. So as we do some soul-searching, we are trying to find out what the truth is for ourselves. When it comes to one Christian sitting with another, so the souls respond, the God parts touching, helping, sharing. One of the great classics of the twentieth-century psychotherapy world is Carl Rogers' book *On Becoming a Person*. It is in such a work and in the writings of an author like that that we begin to see the overlapping of the worlds of the soul in spiritual terms and of the person in psychological terms.

I sniff a dualism here in my own writing. If there is a God part, are there parts of us which are not God's: the body for example? Do we degrade the body, neglect it and only concentrate on the soul? This is a big subject, but, briefly, we are very much integrated people, and one part of us affects another very easily. A toothache can dampen our enthusiasm for life, but pain and suffering does funny things to the soul. It frequently strengthens it, and the soul in response to pain can be quite wise, because there are some pains which are generated by the way we live, think and behave, and the soul in its wisdom can spot this and check it. The body is, at its best, integrated into the life of the soul. Most of us have a long way to go with this integration, but the body is not to be separated. Jesus said 'Take this; this is my body' (Mark 14.22). There is a sense here that his body was a crucial part of himself, and his destiny. It was not in the least to be scorned or rejected, but to be healed and restored and brought back into alliance with the soul, and with his disciples through the memory.

Expertise on the ways of the soul defy professionalism as we understand it today: clear answers, definite codes of practice, certificates, value for money. 'The greatness of such work', wrote Professor Nikos Nissiotis, at one time Director of the Ecumenical Institute at Bossey in Switzerland, 'lies in the fact that one acts not as a professional but as one who must try his best and try harder and harder to fulfil a vocation which is continually overwhelming one.'

The third question I set myself to answer is the one about assessment. How do we know if we are doing it well, and who is to say? 'It' being those times when two people are together, one with the responsibility of offering prayer and spiritual counsel, in an acknowledged setting of support. Occasions of healing in the New Testament which were accompanied with prayer are easily assessed by the effectiveness of their cure, but what about those occasions when it is not healing but self-understanding that is required? How do we assess success here? The Prodigal Son came to himself without the help of a minister. He helped himself. He was his own success. The situations most applicable to the subject in hand are those when Jesus is with another and responding to a question or a request, or entering into dialogue with a troubled soul. To the request of James and John that they should sit with Jesus in glory (Mark 10.35), Jesus helps them to see the need for suffering, as a preliminary to glory. The dialogue situations, the woman at the well, the busy Martha, the enquiring Nicodemus, the passionate Magdalen, all these are pastoral encounters in which Jesus, because he was who he was, brought insightful, authoritative words to bear. What would we count success, or the right thing, in these situations? Such criteria seem to skew us away from the essence of the matter. Success would be a deeper seeing, a deeper realization of the authority of Jesus, and a deeper revelation of oneself in relation to God.

Similarly, if we went to an art gallery and someone asked us 'Did you have a successful visit?' the answer would have to be yes if our eyes were opened to see some beautiful or revealing things which touched our inner feelings. It would have to be no if we came out as we went in. Success is not marks out of ten, it is about seeing and hearing. Those qualities Jesus, echoing Isaiah, often lamented that people did not take further and deeper: 'they may look and look, but see

71

nothing; they may listen and listen, but understand nothing' (Mark 4.12).

If perceiving is the end result, and this often happens by just listening to what one says to another, or does not say, then prayer is helpful in two ways. Spoken prayer can gather together the broken pieces of our perceptions, it can recapitulate the labyrinthine discussion. Unspoken prayer, the presence of the Holy Spirit, can cleanse perception, it can wipe the spectacles clear of misunderstanding, it can move us along towards seeing God and seeing the world as God sees it, and seeing ourselves as God sees us. Prayer is the presence of Christ in all his wisdom, in our own rather feeble attempts at soul-making. Christ is the light in the room, and the light in the mind.

The ancient and familiar artistic device of the halo could be considered an 'assessment' of a Christian's success. That puts it rather crudely, but the presence of light has been a sign of God's favour and presence, ever since glory ricochetted round Bethlehem at the birth of Christ, and long before that in the burning bush. It can be a disarming sight, as Peter found on the Mount of the Transfiguration when Jesus was conversing with Moses and Elijah (Mark 9.5). The Transfiguration has its echoes in the receiving of the stigmata by St Francis of Assisi on Mount La Verna, witnessed by Brother Leo: 'Full of wonder, Brother Leo raised his eyes and saw a lovely and radiant torch of fire descend from heaven, and come to rest over the head of St. Francis' (Third Consideration of the Holy Stigmata of St Francis). More English, and domestic, is Matthew Arnold's description of Newman's preaching on a Sunday afternoon in St Mary's, Oxford:

Who could resist the claim of that spiritual apparition, gliding in the dim afternoon light through the aisles of St. Mary's rising into the pulpit, and then, in the most entrancing of voices breaking the silence with words and thoughts that were a religious music — subtle, sweet, mournful.

Again, Scott Holland describes Edward King, Bishop of

Lincoln, in the nineteenth century, in which King's beauty of character is itself a sermon:

> It was light he carried with him – light that shone through him – light that flowed from him. The room was lit into which he entered. It was as if he had fallen under a streak of sunlight, that flickered and danced, and laughed and turned all to colour and to gold. Those eyes of his were an illumination. (Henry Scott Holland, *A Bundle of Memories*)

There are many other descriptions of the place of light in assessing the proximity to God of his servants. Light cannot be bottled, or pinned to the table, or owned. It will always be a symbol of enlightenment, and illumination of the mind as well as the body. It will not do as currency in the market-place and can never pass an exam, but it is understood and felt by those who are looking for God in this world, and such enlightened souls will be sought out to share that light. Christ said 'I am the light of the world' (John 8.12). St John's Gospel is full of the science of light. We bask in it. We stand in the reflected glory of it.

Prayer is the voice of desire.
St Thomas Aquinas

5

Intercessory prayer

i Praying for others

The world often seems so remarkable, and people so particular and lovable, that it is difficult to know what to do with
the emotion they arouse. I am going to let that unusual optimism stand just for a while. Darkness and despair often seem
to be unfairly weighted in writings and discussion about most
things, but particularly when it comes to praying for others.
There are a lot of overwhelmingly positive experiences which
arise from being in and looking at the natural world: 'The
world is charged with the grandeur of God', wrote Gerard
Manley Hopkins. Also within the realm of human nature,
there is so much that makes us reel in wonder and causes us
to give thanks. This excess of emotion that is aroused by
wonder is often understood to be the mainspring of poetic
creativity. You are in love, you write a poem. That still remains
a real possibility, but love of this overwhelming sort also gets
channelled into relationships, and, far from being sentimental
about it, we find ourselves having to sort out the levels on
which this works for us and for the other. Growing seems to
me a matter of fitting your passions into reasonable channels.
Romantic love sets relationships off, which then need to be
tempered by commitment and realism. I start off this chapter
on intercession by allying it to passion, because I often feel that
intercessions are considered the driest of the forms of prayer,
not helped in recent years by the growing length of them in
public prayer. Praying for people is one way of keeping in
touch with reality, because there is nothing so roundly, and

sometimes so sharply, real as people. There is nothing as beautiful as people, and on the other hand 'ther's nowt as queer as fowk!'

Intercession can be the creative outcome of our desires. Perplexed by what to do for others, when we feel unable to move forward with our passion in any other way, we turn to God and pray for them. The way of the world is such that complete absorption into beauty becomes impossible. We cannot for ever and completely own somebody that is not us, although that is what beauty makes us want. We get into a situation of restlessness, which can only really be satisfied, as St Augustine put it, when we rest in God. So our prayer is a placing of the things and people who move us very deeply into the heart of God. That sense of wanting to own, or to absorb completely, the other, be it a person or a place, is transformed into an offering, a thanksgiving, a petition. We ask God to take over. It is too much for us. We offer our stirred hearts to God, for peace and for understanding.

To develop that easy conversation, the trust in the ever-present reality of God often begins with an uncensored, childlike chatter. When people begin to want to talk to God and to ask God for help about things, one obstacle that needs to be overcome is the problem of what one should ask God for. Are there any rules or etiquette in the process? The simple answer to that is that in the beginning there should be no restraints. God is there to receive our prayers in whatever form they come, and in whatever language, either stumbled out in words of one syllable or in the most beautiful seventeenth-century prose. At the tentative first stages of getting to know God and opening up to him in prayer I think anything goes, there are no silly questions. We can ask God for whatever we want. There should be no barriers, no special protocol, no right dress or posture. 'In everything make your requests known to God in prayer and petition with thanksgiving' (Philippians 4.6). We get so up-tight about being correct with God that often we never get started. If it is a bike we want then it is a bike we ask for. If it is a million pounds on the lottery then we say that to God, as a first stage.

As we go on in this prayer of asking, then inevitably we make various modifications. We get wise to the lack of response from God and ponder why that should be. Why is God not giving me my bike, or the million on the lottery? Perhaps he does not want me to have them. Perhaps he has got something better for me in the future. Perhaps he does not work like that anyway, like a departmental store manager responding to customer demand. We learn to have a different image of what might be going on, and adapt our prayer accordingly, but that is our decision and the result of our experience. We learn through our mistakes.

In the prayer of asking, the picture is more like a parent responding to requests from a child out of limited resources. We can only get from our parents what there is to give, and we often only receive what it seems right for parents to provide. We begin to discover that there is a moral element at work. There are things which God has it in his power to give, and there are things which it is in his nature to want us to have. We learn what those things are as we learn to know God, and although it is important that we do not censor out things too soon, imagining that we know God better than we do, we shall find that a rapport builds up, an empathy in which we discover that God knows what it is we want before we ask it, but he wishes to be involved in the request as a joint enterprise. God does not 'need' prayer, but he does want it.

Someone we know and love is ill with cancer. To ask God to make them better is an entirely understandable prayer. God knows that this is what you want, but what sort of a God is it that you are talking to? Is it a God who is able to step in and remedy each individual need, or is it a God who has created a world in a particular way, which includes limitations on one level, but limitless love on another? Our prayer might turn from expecting personal treatment in the practical human sphere to a request that the person who is ill is brought into the sphere of limitless love, which will make a request for bodily recovery take a lesser place, however heart-rending that may seem at the time. Intercession is eventually a moving alongside God in a partnership of will, and in the act of humility of declaring God's will to be sufficient. Our prayer becomes not what I want, but 'Your will, O God, and help me to bear it.' 'Not my will, but yours, be done.'

So intercession, on one level, draws near to contemplation. It is a way of seeing people, and placing them at the source of Love. This source, or wellspring, is something, over time, you have got to know, and which you trust and wish to share with another. We are not praying for someone who is outside God's care and love, nor are we praying outside God's care and love ourselves; we are entering into a relationship with both God and the other person in a solidarity of care and concern. We do not pray for someone imagining that we are the strong one and they the weak, with God hovering somewhere in between. We are all beggars before God, and God also has shown himself vulnerable and human in Jesus Christ. We do not pray from a position of super health for the sick, or from super strength for the weak; we enter into a relationship with them, with God, and rest in that. In that relationship many questions remain unanswered. There is sometimes a limit in our desire to say 'why?' We just want to rest in the fact that something is, and trust that God who made us is also at the point where something just is. The relentless 'why?' gives way to a simple trust.

How does our original question look now: 'Are there right things to ask for?' Asking has been modified into sharing our mutual need. Words of asking have been reduced by the tangible experience of being held, and we have begun to look more carefully at the God we are with in our intercessory prayer. God is neither ignoramus nor super-power, he is someone with whom we share our needs, trusting that his love will meet them. Set in that context some practical matters about the prayer of asking take on a new light, and one is praying for people we do not know personally.

I said at the beginning of the chapter that our experience of the beauty of the world and of people can have within it a real frustration. We are limited in what we can achieve by our own energy and activity. At times all we can do is offer to pray. We get a fleeting glimpse of someone who were it not for the fact that we have never seen them before could be our sister or brother, the sense of recognition or belonging is so strong. But they pass, they get off the train, they leave the theatre, they disappear into the crowd. Our human limitations of time and space, and capacity to belong, mean we glimpse others and see their potential to be our brothers or sisters, but have no opportunity to go deeper.

We live in a place for a number of years and then move away, unable to keep in touch with all, but God knows each one and each hair of each one's head. Through God's mediation, or in God's large-roomed heart, we share a common humanity with all, and that goes for the evil as well as the good. As we are with God so we are with the whole of humanity. Rather than being nostalgic about the fleeting glimpse and the moving away from those we might never see again, we can bring them into our prayers. Or with those we admire, when we are unable to express our admiration directly, or those who have been kind to us (perhaps they have done something as simple as pick up the shopping when we have fallen down, or something as crucial as deliver us as babies into the world) – we can bring all of these before God in our prayers. If we do not know their names then 'the woman in the supermarket' or 'the one we saw on television last night' will do, for underlying the roll-call of strange names is the reality in which all of humanity is held in God's care. When we pray for them we are also praying with them, with God.

We do this not just because we need to, out of a sense of duty, but because we want to. It gives us the greatest joy to do it. We are saying 'I want to be with that person in their pain, their beauty, their vulnerability, their talent.' We cannot possess others, nor should we want to, nor should we stalk them emotionally out of our own need and loneliness, but we are with them within the love of God. Prayer, in this sense, could be seen as constructing an aerial bridge where we can walk together and everyone, although remaining themselves, feels compassion for each other.

Many people keep an intercession list and find it helpful. A teacher once told me that her list was so long it prevented her from getting to school on time, and a priest who lived for many years in Sheffield, Alan Ecclestone, who was much regarded for his work as a parish priest, kept an ever-increasing intercession list all his life. At his death it had about four hundred names on it. It was part of his attempt to say thank you. It taught him:

> to see our personal lives not as pitiful threads soon to be snapped and forgotten — but as threads woven into an amazing tapestry of life. To pray is to try and extend that emotion, to come back to it, and to deepen it. This practice teaches us indebtedness.

Intercession cannot always be a joy, and sometimes it has to be a duty. The people who drain us of time and energy, the cruel and thoughtless and unloving ought also to be on our lists, to fulfil the new commandment. Praying for our enemies, praying for those who really are a thorn in the flesh to us, praying for the one which every parish has, is the Olympic Games of prayer and self-sacrifice. Not many of us are up to it. Thérèse of Lisieux had such saintly desires that she seemed to have a way to conquer the real pain of sitting next to someone in chapel who sniffs or fidgets, but even for her it was a great trial. That in a way seems to pale into insignificance when we consider Jews praying for their enemies in the concentration camps, but it was done.

Children love to list intercessions and very often they get rattled off. But after years of rattling off, who knows whether through its deep ingrainedness it sometimes gets prayed through more deeply. To go through the act of writing a name down can be very significant. I have a table on which all the requests for prayer are put and they lie there looking pretty unloved most of the time, but, oddly, they seem to shift in the night, as if one of the bits of paper was saying to another 'your turn now' or 'you go first'. A name comes to the top, crying out for attention, and some of the scraps of paper, bits of envelopes or a torn-out bit of diary on which I first wrote the name and the problem, have stayed there for years, defying all tidying up or chucking out.

I was heartened to read that this intuitive approach was also the way of Father William of Glasshampton. William Sirr (1862–1937) was a member of the Society of the Divine Compassion, and attempted to found a contemplative order for men at Glasshampton in Worcestershire. The community did not succeed, but his personal influence over many was profound. Gilbert Shaw writing about Father William's intercessory work put it like this:

> He never lost touch with the world. Through those who came, through an extensive correspondence, and through the many intercessions sent to him, he was alive to the general trend of the passing times. He always kept time for intercession in the inner chapel of Reservation, the time from Vespers until the evening collation. The desk before the altar was piled with correspondence and requests for prayer, for everything as it came having been read and considered, was placed there. Occasionally he might look over it to refresh his memory, but for the most part he knelt motionless giving himself to God in intercession for the reconciliation of men's failures and the strengthening of their good intentions. For him prayer was to be in the will of God. Each request or matter referred to in correspondence or brought to his notice was then and there offered in prayer, so that as he said, 'I carry them on my heart and so in every offering, in Eucharist, in Office, in times of prayer and work I am continually offering them, but in the time set apart for intercession I offer myself particularly for all that has been brought to me and for all for which God would use the devotion of my will.'

One other practical thing about intercessions is that we need to check our categories occasionally. We can get into a rut with the categories and they need to be looked at and refreshed: widows and orphans might make some widows feel pigeon-holed; the elderly, who are they? the sick, are we not sick too? We also have to check with intercessions that

we are not being patronizing or glib, or jumping onto a fash-
ionable bandwagon, or praying too much for bishops and
not enough for school caretakers, or vice versa. One startling
category that I found recently in Lancelot Andrewes' prayers
was for 'those who have been scandalized by me'. Out of an
old leather-bound prayer book in church fell, recently, a piece
of paper, probably from the 1850s, asking the congregation to
pray for 'our suffering fellow subjects in India now grievously
afflicted by plague and famine'.

Jesus' categories for intercession are illuminating: 'pray for
your persecutors' (Matthew 5.44). Jesus prayed for those who
put him on the cross, not knowing what they were doing
(Luke 23.34). He prayed for his disciples, particularly Peter,
'that his faith may not fail'. This seems to be a case where
the will of God does not provide an immediate answer to
prayer, but delays, to increase faith through failure and denial.

One of Jesus' categories for prayer is perplexing. In John
17.9 he says, 'I pray for them [the disciples], I am not praying
for the world.' The world these days is a common area for
intercessions, and quite rightly so. As we receive more and
more information about the world scene, we feel it ought to
be the subject of our prayers. One difficulty here is that many
people assume that God is so old fashioned he does not have
television or radio and needs to be told at length all about
things. Here there seem to be two conflicting messages. Jesus'
message in St John's Gospel, 'I do not pray for the world', and
the contemporary desire to offer the world's problems up to
God on an ever-increasing scale.

In St John's Gospel, Jesus is praying at the very intersection
of the heavenly Kingdom and the world of sin and faithless-
ness. The disciples who have declared their love and shown
their faith must not be allowed to lapse at the last, because
when Jesus has returned to the Father they will have a special
mission to the world. They will have the responsibility to love
the world back into faithfulness. No wonder then that Jesus'
prayer at this time concentrates on the needs of the disciples.
God cannot be accused of being disinterested in the world.
Far from it: 'God so loved the world that he gave his only

Son, that everyone who has faith in him may not perish but have eternal life' (John 3.16).

We pray for the world, but how do we ensure that prayers are not sermons or news bulletins? As in all intercession we need to begin with a clear understanding of the place of God in it all. God loves his creation and grieves over its sin and failure, we share with him in that. God longs for it to be more peaceful, just, loving, more wholesome and less divided, and we can enter into that too. As we address our public intercession to God we need to be clear without being effusive, compassionate without being gushing, informative to the congregation, because they need to have their imaginations kindled, but we must not assume that God is ignorant of the situation. As intercessors we need to come to an ever-closer understanding of God. That is the first priority. From that follows the requests, the tone, the length and the sensitivity towards what are appropriate ways of praying for others, and for situations, both publicly in church and privately in our homes and in small prayer groups.

ii Christ as intercessor

The individual's heroic quest for salvation goes on. We have been given this amazing sense of self which can do things independently of everyone else, and will have to die independently. So it is inevitable that we feel the duty, the responsibility, to respond personally to God. But no one came into the world on their own initiative, and no one is sustained in it entirely on their own. Prayer in solitude (and here I make two quite large leaps that will have to be teased out) joins the prayer of the Church, and that prayer is linked with the prayer of Jesus Christ.

We know the prayer of solitude, the feeble fumblings to talk to God and to listen to God in the silence of our own rooms. We know the many distractions, the picture that needs straightening, the dusting, the rearrangement of books, the letters that lie on the desk unanswered, the fidgeting, the dropping of the book, the looking for the pen. We know all that and it is very distressing, the fly, the digging up of the road outside, the radio in the other room, and occasionally, very occasionally that momentary sense of peace or insight in which the wings of God brush past, or his kiss of peace leaves us stunned but deeply content. That is a reasonably well-defined, tangible experience.

To go on to say that that prayer, however feeble, joins the prayer of the Church is less clearly defined. The prayer of other people who make up the Church is, I imagine, going on at this moment somewhere in the world. Our fleeting attempt to add to that swell of prayer, or chain of prayer as it is sometimes called, slowly builds up the power of prayer throughout the world. In prayer we join with others, even though we do not pray physically with another, since prayer knows no physical boundaries. It gets in and around, and is able to link up through prison walls, across oceans and, many believe, beyond death. However important our own efforts seem to us we should remember that we are part of a much larger process that stretches across centuries and through time.

That prayer of the Church then takes another journey, and here we really are floating in air. It travels to the only one who can present our prayer to God the Father, and that is the Son, Jesus Christ. The idea is familiar to us from St John's Gospel, in which there is a very clear hierarchy of communication, with the Holy Spirit acting as an intermediary, or messenger. It is also an idea which is important to the writer of the letter to Hebrews:

> Jesus holds a perpetual priesthood, because he remains for ever. That is why he is able to save completely those who approach God through him, since he is always alive to plead on their behalf. (Hebrews 7.24, 25)

'To make intercession for them' is the Authorized Version's phrase for 'to plead on their behalf'. There is something of the language of the court or the palace in these texts, and we may not be entirely at home in such places and feel that it is strained as an image. It is not dramatic enough, not humble enough for the Jesus we know who 'went about among us, and stretched out his arms for us on the cross'. It is a case really of how you picture it yourself, and what has real meaning for you. There are pictures, there is what you believe to be true, and what you have made your own.

Jesus can be seen as an intimate friend, who listens to all we say and in his infinite wisdom and patience conveys our requests to God, who is our propitiator, our pleader, our advocate, and has power to effect change. We can understand Jesus as the listening ear, as the one who really does hear and understand. We can see Jesus as the glorious victor on the cross who draws out our inmost needs, and, as the divine one, transforms those needs through his love into a reality which is the best for us. All those fine pictures are dependent on a resonance of image: advocate, listener, conqueror. But how do I really feel it? What is going on in my prayers and in our prayer that resonates with the ancient tradition that Jesus is the listening ear of God and the affective intercessor? Literally, how do I pray? What am I like when I am in the presence of God?

Reading the accounts of others who try and explain what it is like to be with God, there seems to be a whole variety of different responses. At one time Moses only saw God's back; Elijah was aware of his whispering voice, Ezekiel his flying machine, Paul the voice that pierced his conscience, St Teresa of Avila the sword that pierced her heart: all different, but all compelling and all embracing experiences that claim the whole life. Jesus comes to us, looks at us and says, 'yes'. We pray to him, and with him, because he seems to be the most loving person to pray to. I wish I could flood the page with quotations that say more authoritatively what I am struggling to say. To say Christ is the intercessor above all others is not to take it out of the range of the heart, but to reflect the real desire of people to talk to Jesus, because he understands and is doing that understanding with God, as God.

As I move from the vestry into the church for a service, I take a last look at the crucified one and remember that he knows all about the hazards of public speaking; it gives me

85

strength. Confronted by the thunderbolt of tragic news, who else seems, in his purity and power, better to be with? Who knows more than he does about the secrets on the other side of suffering and death? Who else has risen from the dead in such a way as to give hope and comfort and promise to the world? 'He sits at the right hand of God' may be felt as a culturally conditioned image resonant of the government of kings and worldly monarchs, or it may be felt to be a much warmer and homelier picture as we bunch together for warmth in a tent, or sit tightly in a crowded bar, or devoutly kneel beside each other in a time of prayer. 'On the right hand' means close, intimate.

As we gaze upon Jesus, the very thought of motion is lost. It is not we who have forsaken worldly things, but they have dropped away from us. 'They saw no man any more, but Jesus only.' If we are really gazing upon him, then all is well, even though we may perhaps seem to be resting. We are quite unaware that He is transporting us in ecstasies of motion far more powerful than any we have gone through before. Time was when we thought we should get our own way by being busy, but gazing upon Jesus is, indeed, the only progressive power of the soul. (R. M. Benson)

Blessing

God bless Mummy. I know that's right.
Wasn't it fun in the bath to-night?
The cold's so cold, and the hot's so hot.
Oh! God bless Daddy – I quite forgot.

A. A. Milne, 'Vespers'

6

Blessing

One summer morning in a spare half hour before chapel on Sunday at school, I took outside a copy of Wordsworth's poetry. Life was all right. The poets were giving me great support and enjoyment. Against the grain of the contemporary culture, I was valuing the services at school and was thinking I should like to be a clergyman. I read from *The Prelude*:

> Oh there is blessing in this gentle breeze,
> A visitant that while it fans my cheek
> Doth seem half-conscious of the joy it brings.

Holidays in the Lake District had given me an idea of the setting in which that feeling might have arisen. The blessings that nature brings and the blessings of the Holy Spirit were at that time very much coming together for me. That God was good and his world the beneficiary of that goodness was a firm conviction of mine. I realize now that my life was very sheltered and privileged, and no wonder life looked good from my vantage point. But the essential goodness of God, the consciousness of his blessing, has stayed with me through the upheavals and the grief of much that followed that summer's morning before chapel. That was a moment of prayer which has set the tone for all that has followed. It was a blessing, and so when I come up for air and think about prayer on a very basic level, I tend to imagine 'a power for good'. This is a warm beneficence which radiates from a good intent within the soul. Blessings very much come into this category, and blessings in the first place work on a very simple level.

Think of the language. Some phrases have got into the

language and we use them quite automatically, often unaware of their deeper meaning: for example, 'bless you', 'count your blessings' and 'goodbye', which means 'God be with you'. These simple sayings hold within them a history, deeper than their common use would suggest. Blessings are a very ancient form of prayer which we use often unconsciously, but when we use them with the full meaning behind them they can, and should, be very powerful.

It occasionally comes to me strongly at the end of a long Sunday that the last act of Evening Prayer, except saying 'goodbye' to the congregation at the door, is to have the privilege of blessing them, and to trust that it will, through the grace of God, have a beneficial effect. So also in the home and at the bedside a blessing can be given in the knowledge that a benediction, 'a good saying', a word with God's authority, will light up a dark world, a difficult situation.

Rather removed from the Wordsworthian glow is the history of blessings. This can be traced in Scripture and, in particular, in two different strands of thought concerning the authority of who it was that could give a blessing. If we look at the Old Testament we see in the earliest chapters of Genesis, which contain some of the most ancient traditions, blessings being given and shared simply. Those involved in the giving are people honoured by God but who have no particular sacred function. Noah, for example, was a man who 'walked with God', and he called on the Lord to bless the tents of Shem (Genesis 9.26). Noah's authority to bless came from God's prior blessing of him; 'God blessed Noah and his sons.' In the creation story in Genesis 1 God blessed the man and the woman he had made.

The idea of 'original blessing', popular in our own day, has been drawn from this biblical emphasis. It stands in contrast to the more widely held view of original sin. It is interesting, with the growth of support for the idea of God's original blessing, that we think of God as someone who first blesses rather than judges. This is often connected with the idea that the world and nature, not only human beings, are also originally blessed, and ties in with Wordsworth's view that nature is a window onto God. This blessing is a natural birthright, and God's blessing stays very close to the surface of things. This is particularly true of the Celtic tradition, for example in this blessing:

> Deep peace of the running wave to you
> Deep peace of the flowing air to you
> Deep peace of the quiet earth to you
> Deep peace of the shining stars to you
> Deep peace of the Son of peace to you.
>
> (Celtic Traditional)

We are conscious in these blessings that it is God's original blessing of his world and of us that makes us able to call on his blessing and to offer it to others. We do not originate the blessing, but there is a mutuality in it. Hear the mutuality twisting its way round in this piece of writing from St Paul:

> Praise be to the God and Father of our Lord Jesus Christ, the all-merciful Father, the God whose consolation never fails us. He consoles us in all our troubles, so that we in turn may be able to console others in any trouble of theirs and to share with them the consolation we ourselves receive from God. (2 Corinthians 1.3–4)

We are blessed by God so that we in turn can bless. We are comforted so that we in turn can comfort. The initiative is always God's. The strength is always God's. It is easy to drop into a legalistic turn of mind, and to forget the great blessings showered on us indiscriminately by God: 'only so can you be children of your heavenly Father, who causes the sun to rise on good and bad alike' (Matthew 5.45). We can also remember those blessings which we, in particular, have received through no merit of our own. There is no cause for boasting in our ability to bless, but for humility in being called to do so and an acknowledgement of where the original power to bless comes from.

As God is present in all things, so we can draw out from anything that lives a blessing. 'Everything that lives', said William Blake, 'is holy.' As we draw out a blessing from things, so we put back a blessing into them. We bless things by our careful and loving use of them, even the most ordinary things of life, especially the most ordinary things of life. We find ourselves participating in a cycle of blessing. That interpenetration of human and natural things with the divine blessing was much more a part of life before modern living dug a trench between the natural and the holy. The holiness of the natural world, and the natural relationship that by being human we had with God, made the blessing a common way of prayer.

This cycle of blessing is thrillingly expressed in words of the poet Gerard Manley Hopkins. He is walking home after a fishing trip in the Vale of the Elwy at harvest time. His heart and the presence of God in the landscape begin to fill each other, so that they become mutually blessed. 'These things' that Hopkins refers to are clouds, stooks and especially the hills:

> These things, these things were here and but the
>   beholder
> Wanting; which two when they once meet,
> The heart rears wings bold and bolder
> And hurls for him, O half hurls earth for him off
>   under his feet.
>   (from 'Hurrahing in Harvest')

We must not imagine such ease of divine–human communication through blessing came out of a state of blissful living. It came probably out of an equally real sense of darkness and fear, violence, sickness and death. We want to bless and be blessed because we know the horror of a world unblessed.

Being asked to bless a car I faltered, until I realized that the request came out of an experience in which the previous car had crashed and there was tragic loss of life. In blessing a car we are not doing magical things to metal and plastic, we are placing something that can so easily be an instrument of destruction into the area of God's goodness and patience, and through the tangible and material things of life, helping people learn compassion, skill and patience, in the presence of God. Objects that we use in daily life can be used or abused. A blessing holds what seems so ordinary in the warmth of God's presence. The natural blessings of the Celtic tradition over fire, water, earth, animals, doors, hearths, bedtime, getting up, children, journeys, all acknowledge the thin veil between the ordinary and the divine.

The Celtic 'lorica' prayers which ask God to protect parts of the body from the wiles of the devil are on similar lines. A lorica is a corselet or cuirass of leather, a protective garment, and has given its name to a series of prayers, the most famous being St Patrick's Lorica or Breastplate. In our own day when the body is taking such an important part in our spirituality the lorica could come again into its own as a prayer form. Sitting cross-legged listening to a Theravada Buddhist teacher taking us through the parts of our body in meditation has strong connections with the Celtic tradition. Both are willing God to be present in the incarnate, and, more valuable, calling God out from the depth of our incarnate being, letting our instinctive godliness flourish.

In the Genesis narrative this history of blessing continues, but there are twists and turns. Everybody is blessed through the first people created: 'God created human beings in his own image; in the image of God he created them; male and female he created them. God blessed them and said to them, "Be fruitful and increase"' (Genesis 1.27, 28). This blessing is set back by the failure of people to live up to that blessed state, typified in the temptation of the Garden of Eden. As a result, we have to win back the blessing of God, which Christ did supremely for us on the cross. In the Old Testament, also, there were people who God blessed because they showed faith.

Abraham, through his faith in God, is blessed by the priest-king, Melchizedek:

> Blessed be Abram by God Most High,
> Creator of the heavens and the earth,
> And blessed be God Most High,
> who has delivered your enemies into your hand.
> (Genesis 14.19–20)

What develops in the tradition, is an increasing tightness around the privilege of being able to bless. Only those who were ritually clean, or who had been particularly set aside, or chosen to be a member of the priestly caste, were able to bless. The famous blessing of Aaron in Numbers is given through Moses to Aaron. The authority is handed on. This handing on comes after a long chapter about ritual purity, and about the divining of who or who was not an adulteress. Definitions, groups, those in, those out, meant a lot to a certain religious section of Hebrew society, but the words of that blessing, regardless of the religious politics, are very beautiful and are still used today:

> The Lord said to Moses, 'Say this to Aaron and his sons: These are the words with which you are to bless the Israelites:
>
> > May the Lord bless you and guard you;
> > may the Lord make his face shine on you
> > and be gracious to you;
> > may the Lord look kindly on you and
> > give you peace.
>
> So they are to invoke my name on the Israelites, and I shall bless them.'
>
> (Numbers 6.22–27)

Alongside this increasingly priestly preserve of blessing, ran, in the Jewish tradition, the common practice of the mother and father of the family assuming the priestly role for their own family. The father blesses the Passover meal on the Sabbath, and calls down blessings on his family for all sorts of things. The mother blesses the light and the candles. This is again taken up informally by the younger members of the family, rather like saying grace, and the children bless things too. There is a yiddish saying, 'His granddaughter already knows how to say the bracha [blessing] for eating fruit.' That is not surprising, because the sooner it is blessed, the sooner she can get on and eat it! Saying blessings in recognition of the Divine blessing is one of the most ingrained of traditional

94

Jewish customs. The blessing over the wine, the blessing for eating bread, cereals, vegetables, fruit, the blessing for seeing the blossoms of spring, and, the hardest one to say, the blessing on hearing tragic tidings.

Jesus, unauthorized in the Pharisaic sense, but obviously with some rabbinic, or teacher status behind him, blessed children, he blessed the bread and the wine at the Last Supper as Lord over his disciples, he blessed Simon Peter (Matthew 16.17), and it was his final act as recorded by St Luke: 'Then he led them out as far as Bethany, and blessed them with uplifted hands; and in the act of blessing he parted from them' (Luke 24.50–51). What is quite unusual in the Gospels is for anyone other than Jesus to bless. There is, though, a reference to Simeon, a representative of faithful Israel, blessing Joseph and Mary as they came into the Temple to present Jesus to God. What is most interesting is that when Jesus grew up he radically redefined the category of the blessed. They were to be the poor, the meek, the merciful, those who thirst after justice, and he admonished his disciples to bless those who curse them.

Certainly, through Christian history, the privilege, the commission to bless, has been jealously guarded by the apostolic succession of bishops who have handed on that commission to the clergy through ordination. The blessing has been very much the preserve of the clergy in the services of the Church, in the sacraments and in pastoral work. That cannot easily be forgotten or written out, or put aside, but where does that leave the lay people who visit on behalf of the clergy? Are they able to bless or not?

George Herbert, in his classic work of pastoral practice, *The Country Parson*, strikes a very serious note on blessing when he writes:

> Now blessing differs from prayer, in assurance, because it is not performed by way of request, but of confidence, and power, effectually applying God's favour to the blessed, by the interesting of that dignity wherewith God hath invested the Priest, and ingaging of God's own power and institution for a blessing.

What he is saying here is that it is a particular legal entitlement, an 'interesting' (what he should expect to be most interested in), an 'interesting' of the priest, to bless. Herbert criticizes those who are more inclined just to use the familiar worldly greetings, or do not see the need at all for blessings. He heightens the profile of blessing, but still definitely within the orbit of the priest's function. He says that the priest's neglect of the importance of the blessing has led to the people also neglecting the need for it:

> so that they are far from craving this benefit from their ghostly Father, that they oftentimes go out of church, before he hath blessed them . . . but the Parson first values the gift in himself, and then teacheth his parish to value it.

It is urged by Herbert that it is not the person, as such, who holds the authority to bless, so much as the function he has been given. So you can have a sick or sinful priest and a worthy blessing from them, as for example Eli who was disallowed by God but blessed Hannah. The power and authority to bless comes with ordination. That would seem to be an impasse, and the answer to the question 'Can lay people give a blessing?' is, on a legal basis, 'No'.

Unpacking that role and responsibility we find it hard to understand how the power of conveying God's good will is so confined to a group, regardless of their moral stature or their ability to relate to another person. Could not a lay person, through their prayer and their life with God, convey, mediate, administer God's blessing to another? I mean in the sense that Portia in *The Merchant of Venice* used the term, when she talked about mercy being the agent of God's blessing: 'It is twice blessed, it blesseth him that gives and him that takes.'

In practice I am sure this happens. A nurse or doctor, or a friend can 'be' a blessing in the way they treat you, God working in secret through the good words, benediction, and the good deeds of another. The legality and the binding of orders does provide some sort of safety net against indiscriminate use of unauthorized and unworthy power, but in the

Jewish sense a blessing receives its authority first from God and then through the moral and spiritual integrity of the one who gives the blessing. It is possible for anyone to discover for another the blessings that lie all around, and that rest particularly in the Creator.

Having said that, the power vested in it reminds the clergy of the immense privilege of the act of blessing, and the laity of the utter seriousness with which the Church takes the power to bless. In medieval times, a blessing was considered one of the best ways to heal a person, and a blessing with the laying on of hands is still an essential aspect of Christian healing. The clergy are set aside for this work and maintain their lives to justify the honour given them. The laity might consider that their pastoral role is more in the way of natural blessings, the blessings of kindness, and mercy, and in being there, and in listening, and may feel it right, in the absence of a priest, to share a blessing – 'May the blessing of Almighty God be with us' – rather than pronounce a blessing. In the same way, a priest would defer to a bishop's blessing if a bishop were present when a blessing was needed. This sounds a bit legalistic, and I am sure most people would be totally unaware of any distinction as far as words were concerned, but it is a matter of concern for those lay people who are involved in pastoral care and feel the need to draw it to completion by calling on the blessing of God. I hope that I have at least presented a picture which makes the situation understandable.

Meanwhile there are many beautiful domestic blessings which can be used in a neutral way as far as the debate about authority goes, in which we bless each other rather than claim the power to mediate God's blessing. It is a pity we cannot hear Martin Luther King's voice pronouncing this, for he used it in his ministry before his assassination:

And now unto him who is able to keep us from falling and lift us from the dark valley of despair to the bright mountain of hope, from the midnight of desperation to the daybreak of joy; to him be power and authority, for ever and ever.

97

This blessing is from Lancelot Andrewes' *Private Prayers* and is
from Psalm 121:

> The Lord himself be your keeper,
> The Lord be your defence at your right hand,
> The Lord preserve you from all evil,
> Surely the Lord is he who shall keep your soul.
> The Lord preserve your going out
> and your coming in
> from this time forth
> for evermore,
> Amen.

To finish this chapter in the ascendant, and to bring it back
to the blessing of the 'gentle breeze' which began it, here is a
flourish from Lancelot Andrewes, who is to prayer what
Wordsworth is to poetry in the manner of blessings. In one
of the earliest edited editions of Andrewes' prayers, David
Stokes (1591–1669) puts this as a final blessing and calls on
us as readers to listen:

> We are now coming to the incomparable Bishop's last
> hymn, and sweetest Anthem in which he was wont to shut
> up and conclude the devotions of the whole day.
>   Hark! Hark! stand a little and listen, and admire, for it is
> a full Anthem. (*Verus Christianus*, 1668)

(A Blessing of Bishop Lancelot Andrewes from his *Private
Prayers*, translated from the Latin.)

> Blessed are you, Lord God of our forebears,
> creating the changes of the days and nights,
> delivering us from the evil of this day,
> giving us the chance of song in the evening,
> to get us through the night without fear and in hope,
> for you are our light, our salvation and the strength of our life
> of whom then shall we be afraid.

Blessing

Glory be to you, o Lord, Glory be to you,
for all your divine perfection,
for your inexpressible and unimaginable
goodness and mercy
to sinners and the unworthy,
and to me
a sinner, of all the most unworthy,
o Lord,
glory, praise, and blessing and thanksgiving
by the voices and concert of voices,
both of angels and of us,
and of all your saints in heaven
and of all your creatures on earth
and under the earth,
and of me the sinner, unworthy and wretched,
world without end,
Amen.

Nothing in all creation is so like God as stillness.

Meister Eckhart

7

After silence, an Amen

The last of George Herbert's thirty-seven chapters on the priestly life, *A Priest to the Temple*, or *A Country Parson* (1632), is a strangely oblique one. It is not a great fanfare of eloquent praise on how good it is to be a priest, it is called 'Concerning detraction'. Detraction is 'the action of detracting from a person's merit . . . the action of what is injurious to his reputation'. It is about when a priest should speak or keep silent about another. Herbert knew that gossip was the community glue in the country districts, and it obviously concerned him how much he should say and listen with regard to the faults of those in his parish. There is, he says, a precedent in law for bringing to light and exposing the crimes of people, and therefore a priest, without malice or enjoyment, can similarly join in the condemnation of particular law-breakers. The final thought, though, is in a completely different tone, as we have come to expect of Herbert, and it is on silence: 'Nevertheless, if the punished delinquent shall be much troubled for his sins, and turne quite another man, doubtless then also men's affections and words must turne, and forebear to speak of that, which even God himself hath forgotten.' Forbearing to speak because God forebears to speak. We take our turn from God. There are certain areas in ministry when forbearance is the creative option. We must not imagine that we should always have the last word, the right answer, the perfect solution, or indeed the prize for the best pupil. When it comes to dealing with others, very often we sense our limitations, our failure to produce the magic cure, the right word at the right time. We have simply been privileged to listen to and to be alongside another.

The silence of sins forgotten is one area in which eloquence ceases to have power, and the impotence of the cross takes over. There are others. What happens when you simply do not know what to say, or you do not particularly want to say anything? These are two rather distinct areas. There is the perplexing dumbness which comes over us in the presence of overwhelming tragedy, the time of T. S. Eliot's 'unprayable prayer at the calamitous annunciation'. Then there is the other silence when words seem second-best to a shared activity, or simply to a silent presence. Thinking of this shared presence I will risk an anecdote, because it has gone deeply into my memory and is the sort of touchstone by which I guide my understanding of visiting. It was a very hot summer's day and I was visiting an elderly woman. I enjoyed the visits, but it was hot and I was extremely tired, and so was she. It was a very sleepy sort of day. She said she would rather have a nap than do a lot of talking, and I said that I would like a nap too. So for half an hour we snoozed away in our separate armchairs. To share a time of sleep is risky sort of advice to give to anyone on pastoral visiting, but I think it draws out the point that holiness, and prayer, is not always to do with speaking.

God can even pray in you and through you while you sleep. This is what a wise Sister told me when I was on retreat during a rare few days away from a rather hectic curacy and spent most of the time fast asleep. When St Paul writes 'pray always', the prayer he is thinking of is not so much something that is done, but is an acknowledgement of something God does in us, allowing you to be you, and me to be me. The sharing that took place in that particular visit I referred to was a sharing of vulnerability, of being honest and being oneself. Prayer is being ourselves before one another and before God.

Then there is the silence involved in visiting those who are close to their death. A day or two or an hour or two before that moment when people pass through the great mysterious barrier is something which we all stand in awe of, and no one has real expertise in. For many it can be a very peaceful time, not for all, but more frequently than we are often led to believe. Words in such a situation seem to be out of place, too casual, too worldly, too chatty, and so we sit in silence, holding a hand or wiping a brow.

Those who have expertise in these matters say that people who are seemingly unconscious close to death are not always unreceptive to sound. They do hear and understand more than we think. That is why nurses I believe never speak about patients in the third person when they are by their bedsides, or in hearing range. So having said that silence is best, there are words to say, or to read, which can share the nature of the silence, that are audible but do not jar against the reflective peace of oncoming death. A passage from Scripture, from St John's Gospel, or a psalm of comfort or hope, do not cut against the grain of the moment. There is something about being in the presence of death which naturally makes us reflective about our own priorities, our own mortality. Sensing the absurdity of so much of life's expectations and aspirations, and thinking reflectively about the nature of God's Kingdom, is in a strange way allowing the person we are with to be a facilitator and not just a receiver. The silence allows a sense of oneness. We give a loving attention to the person, and read all that their face tells us about them on this last stage of the journey. In a way it is a relief that words are unnecessary, when there is no need to make small talk and words no longer get in the way of a deeper communication. That is the unutterable beauty of silence.

I would like now to turn from the unutterable to the unspeakable – the silence which strikes us at the shock of sudden loss, the inexplicability of accident. What to say at such occasions is a very testing problem. When emotions are highly charged, little things are remembered out of all proportion to their well-intentioned meaning. We can assist or aggravate more easily than in less fraught times. A lot of questions are asked, and a lot of quick sorting out is required as to whether they are rhetorical questions not needing an answer, or whether the grieving person would really value some explanation, as far as it is possible to give it. Explanations simply do not work for some, although for other people going over the details, the retelling of the story, what happened, when, how, how did you feel – the ordinary 'cup of tea' talk – can be as comforting as anything. You have to feel your way with this sort of conversation. It is a bit like flying a kite and having to read the tugs of wind through the string, to know how best to respond, to stand or sit alongside those in tragedy. In silence, we need to be sensitive to the right moment to be there, and the right moment not to be there.

We think of Jesus' passion, and the silence that surrounded that. There were just a few staccato sentences: 'I thirst', 'Father, forgive them', 'Into thy hands, O Lord, I commend my spirit' – just a few phrases coming out of a much greater silence. Our pastoral work is occasionally in those moments of unspeakable tragedy. The experience in our own society of those who have assisted at the tragedies of our times – Aberfan, Hillsborough, Lockerbie, Zeebrügge, Dunblane – will be of help to us all. The wisdom that is emerging from these tragedies is that being able to talk about things is very helpful, and therefore to have willing and sensitive listeners is important.

Then when we have been through those situations with another, we need to return to the silent place from which we set out, which may be our hearts or our rooms, and be with God alone, for the other person. That is the time we refuel with a silent and private offering, back to the generator, to share with God the sadness and the joys we have experienced. So we come full circle: prayer out of silence, into the world to be with other people in their need, learning from them, suffering with them, and back into the silence again. Silence is never an end in itself, for Christians will always be enlivened by the double axis of our faith, loving God and loving our neighbour.

When I was asked, before I was ordained, why I wanted to be a clergyman, I used to draw out of the air an answer which was quite difficult to articulate, although I felt it very strongly.

By being a priest and a pastor, to use both of George Herbert's titles, I felt I could be so many other things as well. There is a little bit of a lot of things in most priests, having to be all things to all people. I felt that the whole world with all its people and all the experiences of it were part of the job. Not exactly the world is my parish, but because God was the creator of all, all things were godly, and therefore everything was part of the life. There would be keys to unlock a lot of doors, even the most undesirable and remote. This promethean approach was the child of thirty years ago, when all things seemed possible. The limitations of life have since become obvious, and while the physical ability to be everywhere at once has gone, the sense of responsibility, interest and curiosity for the whole human enterprise has not. Within an Anglican parish this human enterprise is seen in miniature, and the church with its increasing lay participation and ecumenical fellowship seeks to serve God within its bounds. The Church, if it is to be incarnate as Christ became incarnate, needs to stay in the parishes. We should rejoice to maintain the holy places and to call new holy places into being. We must rejoice in the struggle to serve God in our place, and to serve the people, and to recall them to worship. All sorts of people want to pray. All sorts of people do pray. They seek the moment, and sometimes the moment surprises them. The priest who knows the power and the joy of prayer will find the time and the occasion to practise it, to teach it and to affirm and encourage it in others with a humble but distinct Amen.

The Society for Promoting Christian Knowledge (SPCK) has as its purpose three main tasks:

- **Communicating the Christian faith in its rich diversity**

- **Helping people to understand the Christian faith and to develop their personal faith**

- **Equipping Christians for mission and ministry**

SPCK Worldwide serves the Church through Christian literature and communication projects in over 100 countries. Special schemes also provide books for those training for ministry in many parts of the developing world. SPCK Worldwide's ministry involves Churches of many traditions. This worldwide service depends upon the generosity of others and all gifts are spent wholly on ministry programmes, without deductions.

SPCK Bookshops support the life of the Christian community by making available a full range of Christian literature and other resources, and by providing support to bookstalls and book agents throughout the UK. SPCK Bookshops' mail order department meets the needs of overseas customers and those unable to have access to local bookshops.

SPCK Publishing produces Christian books and resources, covering a wide range of inspirational, pastoral, practical and academic subjects. Authors are drawn from many different Christian traditions, and publications aim to meet the needs of a wide variety of readers in the UK and throughout the world.

The Society does not necessarily endorse the individual views contained in its publications, but hopes they stimulate readers to think about and further develop their Christian faith.

For further information about the Society, please write to:
SPCK, Holy Trinity Church, Marylebone Road,
London NW1 4DU, United Kingdom.
Telephone: 0171 387 5282